RELIGION AND THE U.S. PRESIDENCY

GARLAND REFERENCE LIBRARY
OF SOCIAL SCIENCE
(Vol. 334)

RELIGION AND THE U.S. PRESIDENCY:
A Bibliography

Albert J. Menendez

GARLAND PUBLISHING, INC. • NEW YORK & LONDON
1986

© 1986 Albert J. Menendez
All rights reserved

Library of Congress Cataloging-in-Publication Data

Menendez, Albert J.
  Religion and the U.S. presidency.

  (Garland reference library of social science ;
    vol. 334)
  Includes indexes.
  1. Presidents—United States—Religion—Bibliography.
  I. Title. II. Series: Garland reference library of
    social science ; v. 334.
Z1249.P7M46 1986   016.973′09′92   85-29300
  [E176.1]
  ISBN 0-8240-8718-6

Printed on acid-free, 250-year-life paper
Manufactured in the United States of America

FOR SHIRLEY

ACKNOWLEDGMENTS

Several people helped tremendously in the research for this book. I am indebted to Ann Liu of Duke University, Cindy Russell of Texas Christian University, David Schleicher of Baylor University and Steve Sherrill of Baylor University.

My unfailingly cheerful and skilled secretary Paula Wiley did her usual superlative job in preparing the manuscript for publication. I am grateful to them all.

Albert J. Menendez
October, 1985

CONTENTS

Introduction	xi
The Basic Literature	3
The Presidents:	
John Adams	9
John Quincy Adams	11
Chester Arthur	13
James Buchanan	15
Jimmy Carter	17
Grover Cleveland	23
Calvin Coolidge	25
Dwight Eisenhower	27
Millard Fillmore	31
Gerald Ford	33
James Garfield	35
Ulysses S. Grant	37
Warren Harding	39
Benjamin Harrison	41
William Henry Harrison	43
Rutherford Hayes	45
Herbert Hoover	47

Andrew Jackson	49
Thomas Jefferson	51
Andrew Johnson	59
Lyndon Johnson	61
John F. Kennedy	63
Abraham Lincoln	67
James Madison	77
William McKinley	79
James Monroe	81
Richard Nixon	83
Franklin Pierce	87
James K. Polk	89
Ronald Reagan	91
Franklin D. Roosevelt	103
Theodore Roosevelt	107
William H. Taft	111
Zachary Taylor	113
Harry Truman	115
John Tyler	119
Martin Van Buren	121
George Washington	123
Woodrow Wilson	131
Author Index	135
Subject Index	141

INTRODUCTION

Interest in the religious practices and beliefs of our presidents remains high after a steady stream of "born-again" presidents during the past decade. The Reagan presidency has made religion a high-priority item, and this book has been prepared to help those who are interested in exploring presidential religion in some depth.

After an introductory chapter, citing basic reference works in the field, the book continues with a chapter on each president. For each chief executive, I have included material relating to his personal religion, his relationship with various religious communities and his handling of church-state disputes. For some presidents, e.g., Washington, Lincoln, Jefferson, Carter, Reagan, there is much solid information. But for many others, there is a dearth of material.

It is my hope that this book will stimulate greater interest in a topic of considerable importance to our understanding of the development of the presidency.

RELIGION AND THE U.S. PRESIDENCY

THE BASIC LITERATURE

Several books have attempted to summarize the religious beliefs held by our presidents. Capsule portraits of each president's personal faith and its public relevance have been attempted by John Sutherland Bonnell, Bliss Isely, Vernon Hampton, William Hampton, and Edmund Fuller and David Green. None of these omnibus volumes can be recommended wholeheartedly, but for several presidents they represent the only available information.

Vernon Hampton's Religious Background of the White House is probably a shade better than its competitors because the author was fascinated with anecdotal and comparative material. He tells much about the religious upbringing of the presidents and includes more information about the First Ladies than other volumes. He alone reveals that Hoover's mother was a Quaker preacher, of sorts. Since Quakers do not ordain clergy in the sense that that term is generally used, Hoover has not been classified as a minister's son, as were Cleveland, Arthur, and Wilson.

The Fuller-Green volume, God in the White House, is entertaining and cautious. It does not claim sainthood nor invent religiousness for presidents when adequate data are unavailable. It also attempts a comparison of the religiousness of the presidents.

Isely (Presidents: Men of Faith) tends to be pious but brims with useful information. Bonnell's study (Presidential Profiles) is exceedingly superficial, almost worthless for scholars. Strangely, Bonnell attempts to downgrade the Unitarian and Episcopalian contingent by failing to include several presidents in their appropriate denominational category. (He fails to include either Adams as Unitarian, for example.) His judgments are dubious at best. William Hampton's volume also lacks any redeeming value.

Robert Alley's So Help Me God attempts to classify presidential religious styles with an ingenious interpretive schemata which groups our presidents into three distinct traditions.

One is the Congregationalist-Unitarian mode which is "goal-oriented", humanistic, and "repudiates the restrictive proclivities" of institutional religion. Here we find Jefferson, Madison, Lincoln, and the two Adamses.

Then we have the legalistic Calvinists who propounded and implemented the concept of "American Messianism." Alley says these presidents (Jefferson, Grant, Coolidge, Hoover, Truman, Eisenhower, Johnson, Nixon) believed that "national success was dependent upon national righteousness." These chief executives, he argues, "sought to implement a king's chapel in a king's court without the religious establishment."

Several presidents (Washington, Pierce, Arthur, Franklin Roosevelt, Kennedy) were Anglican-Catholic pragmatic idealists who emphasized realism and situation ethics. They, says Alley, "viewed politics and religion in perfect harmony each with its own sphere," a policy which "allows for freedom in movement from church to state." This approach "takes the institutions of religion seriously, positively." Alley's work is essential for students of presidential religion.

Why should a civil official of a secular state be a high priest or endow himself with quasi-religious functions? This often-noted anomaly of the first nation on earth to separate church and state is analyzed thoroughly by James Fairbanks and Merlin Gustafson. Their stimulating views should be read along with Paul Boller's admirable and concise survey.

Frederic Fox, a Congregationalist pastor who handled religious matters for President Eisenhower, describes the first two decades of the National Day of Prayer, an official act of Congress in 1952 which calls upon the President to proclaim such a day each year. David Kucharsky, a onetime Washington journalist, reviews the history of the Presidential Prayer Breakfasts begun by Eisenhower in 1953. Charles LaFontaine, a Graymoor friar, and Cynthia Toulin analyze the religious content of the presidential inaugural address and draw some startling conclusions. Martin Medhurst traces the inaugural prayer custom while Albert Menendez looks at the homiletical role of presidents from Washington to Reagan. (Only Jefferson and Jackson refused to proclaim days of thanksgiving, prayer, humiliation, and fasting.)

Basic Literature

How religious issues have affected presidential campaigns is found in the volumes by Berton Dulce, Wallace Farnham, Albert Menendez, Peter Odegard and Murray Stedman. Much additional material can be located in <u>Religious Conflict in America: A Bibliography</u> by Albert J. Menendez (New York: Garland Publishing, Inc., 1985). Professor Richard Pierard's study of evangelist Billy Graham's influence on Truman, Eisenhower, Kennedy, Johnson and Nixon is essential reading.

Two odd volumes are worthy of some perusal. Olga Jones surveys the relationships of our presidents to various churches they attended in Washington. J. W. Storer reveals which biblical passages were selected by Presidents Lincoln through Ford at their inaugurations or accessions.

An example of history as propaganda is Franklin Steiner's <u>Religious Beliefs of Our Presidents</u>, published by the distinguished old freethinker house of Haldeman-Julius. Though the publisher assures us that this book is "thoroughly documented, straightforward, and trustworthy," it is nothing of the kind. It is a highly selective attempt to prove the irreligiousness and skepticism of as many presidents as possible. Steiner cites only Herndon, for example, to "prove" that Lincoln was a skeptic, without examining considerable documentation from Lincoln's later life that refutes Herndon. He tries to downgrade Washington's religiousness by showing that our first president rarely received communion in the Anglican/Episcopal church. Anglican historians, however, point out that frequent reception of Holy Communion in the eighteenth century was not the norm and did not become so until well into this century.

Steiner also eliminates five Episcopalian presidents (Madison, Monroe, Tyler, Taylor, Arthur), claiming that their religious views were "doubtful." He includes Polk among the Presbyterians though Polk resolutely refused to join any church until he was baptized by a Methodist preacher on his deathbed. He says Theodore Roosevelt was "not very religious," which is contrary to all evidence.

A half century later, John McCollister suggests in <u>So Help Me God</u> that all of our presidents were deeply pious God-fearing folk, which is just as absurd as Steiner. McCollister includes brief sketches of all presidents, including Reagan, but the amount of worthwhile material in his book would not fill a thimble. About Franklin Roosevelt, for example, he includes about five paragraphs of useless information. McCollister includes lots of pictures, reducing the textbook material to about what a grammar school child could absorb.

1 Alley, Robert S. So Help Me God: Religion and the Presidency, Wilson to Nixon. Richmond: John Knox Press, 1972.

2 Boller, Paul F. "Religion and the U.S. Presidency." Journal of Church & State 21 (Winter 1979): 5-21.

3 Bonnell, John Sutherland. Presidential Profiles: Religion in the Life of American Presidents. Philadelphia: Westminster Press, 1971.

4 Dulce, Berton and Edward J. Richter. Religion and the Presidency. New York: MacMillan, 1962.

5 Fairbanks, James David. "The Priestly Functions of the Presidency." Presidential Studies Quarterly 11 (1981): 214-232.

6 Farnham, Wallace D. "The Religious Issue in American Politics: An Historical Commentary." Queens Quarterly 69 (1961): 47-65.

7 Fox, Frederic. "The National Day of Prayer." Theology Today 29 (July 1973): 258-280.

8 Fuller, Edmund and David E. Green. God in the White House: The Faiths of American Presidents. New York: Crown, 1968.

9 Gustafson, Merlin. "The Religious Role of the President." Midwest Journal of Political Science 14 (November 1970): 708-722.

10 Hampton, Vernon B. The Religious Background of the White House. Boston: Christopher, 1932.

11 Hampton, William Judson. The Religion of the Presidents. Somerville, N.J.: Somerville Press, 1925.

12 Isely, Bliss. Presidents, Men of Faith. Boston: Wilde, 1953.

13 Jones, Olga. Churches of the Presidents in Washington. New York: Vantage, 1961.

Basic Literature

14 Kucharsky, David. "Handclaps and Prayers: Washington Prayer Breakfasts." Christianity Today 16 (February 18, 1972): 53-54.

15 ------. "Prototype of Heaven? Presidential Prayer Breakfasts." Christianity Today 14 (February 27, 1970): 39.

16 LaFontaine, Charles V. "God and Nation in Selected U.S. Presidential Inaugural Addresses, 1789-1945." Journal of Church & State 18 (Winter 1976): 39-60; (Autumn 1976): 503-521.

17 McCabe, Joseph. Seven Infidel U.S. Presidents. Girard, Ks.: Haldeman-Julius, 1927.

18 McCollister, John. So Help Me God. Bloomington, Mn.: Landmark Books, 1982.

19 Medhurst, Martin J. "From Duche to Provoost: The Birth of the Inaugural Prayer." Journal of Church & State 24 (Autumn 1982): 573-588.

20 Menendez, Albert J. "The President as Preacher." Church & State 35 (May 1982): 13-17.

21 ------. Religion at the Polls. Philadelphia: Westminster Press, 1977.

22 Odegard, Peter H., ed. Religion and Politics. Dobbs Ferry, N.Y.: Oceana, 1960.

23 Pierard, Richard V. "Billy Graham and the U.S. Presidency." Journal of Church & State 22 (Winter 1980): 107-127.

24 Stedham, Murray S. Religion and Politics in America. New York: Harcourt, Brace, 1964.

25 Steiner, Franklin. The Religious Beliefs of Our Presidents. Girard, Ks.: Haldeman-Julius, 1936.

26 Storer, J.W. The Presidents and the Bible. Nashville: Broadman, 1976.

27 Toulin, Cynthia. "American Civil Religion from 1789 to 1981: A Content Analysis of Presidential Inaugural Addresses." Review of Religious Research 25

(September 1983): 39-48.

28 Wells, Ronald A. "American Presidents as Political and Moral Leaders: A Report on Four Surveys." Fides et Historia 11 (Fall 1978): 39-53.

JOHN ADAMS

Our second president was a rather independent-minded New Englander who espoused a kind of moderate Christian Unitarianism. But he was fairly tolerant of all creeds. In a letter to Benjamin Rush, dated January 21, 1810, Adams said, "Ask me not whether I am a Catholic or Protestant, Calvinist or Arminian. As far as they are Christians, I wish to be a fellow-disciple with them all."

Adams rejected the Trinity but believed himself to be a Christian. He attended the Episcopal Church during his Presidency after rejecting the strict Congregationalism of his youth. He moved toward Unitarian thought as he continued his deep theological reading. He strongly believed in a future state, an immortality, once telling his friend, Thomas Jefferson, "If I did not believe in a future state, I should believe in no God."

A profound religious thinker, Adams was not really at home in any denominational setting.

The chapter in Norman Cousins' book is a good place to sample the breadth of Adams' religious thought. Both Everettt and Schultz are illuminating. Fuller does a good job of compressing a lot of material into a believable sketch.

See Bonnell, item 3, pp. 26-29.

See Fuller, item 8, pp. 18-27.

See Hampton, V., item 10, pp. 199-203.

See Hampton, W., item 11, pp. 16-20.

See Isely, item 12, pp. 11-16.

29   Cousins, Norman, ed. <u>In God We Trust</u>. New York: Harper, 1958. pp. 74-113.

30 Everett, Robert B. "The Mature Religious Thoughts of John Adams." Proceedings of the South Carolina Historical Association (1966): 49-57.

31 Schulz, Constance B. "The Radical Religious Ideas of Thomas Jefferson and John Adams: A Comparison." Ph.D. dissertation. University of Cincinnati, 1973.

JOHN QUINCY ADAMS

John Quincy Adams rejected the stern Congregationalism of his youth but did not move quite so far toward Unitarianism as his father. He might best be described as an Independent Congregationalist. While living in London, he was wed at All Hallows parish of the Church of England.

Adams read the entire Bible each year, devoting his early morning hours to perusing about five chapters. He wrote voluminous letters and poems about religion to his children, which form the main source of material. The chapter in West's doctoral dissertation is the best summary of Adams' religious beliefs.

See Bonnell, item 3, pp. 50-53.

See Fuller, item 8, pp. 52-59.

See Hampton, V., item 10, pp. 386-389.

See Hampton, W., item 11, pp. 27-30.

See Isely, item 12, pp. 43-48.

32 Adams, John Quincy. An Address to the Catholic Voters of Baltimore. Baltimore: Lucas & Deaver, 1828.

33 ------. Experiences of the Higher Christian Life. New York: Sheldon & Co., 1870.

34 ------. Letters of John Quincy Adams to His Son on the Bible and Its Teachings. Auburn: Alden Beardsley & Co., 1852.

35 ------. "Letter on Scriptures." American Quarterly Register 12 (1839): 86.

36 ------. Letters Upon the Subject of Masonry & Anti-Masonry. Providence: Edward & J.W. Cory, 1833.

37 ------. *Poems of Religion and Society*. Buffalo: Miller, Orton, and Mulligan, 1854.

38 Baker, E.G. "Was He A Unitarian?" *Unitarian Review* 16 (1890): 135.

39 Banks, Louis Albert. *The Religious Life of Famous Americans*. New York: American Tract Society, 1904. pp. 41-52.

40 Gannett, E.S. "Religious Views of John Quincy Adams." *Christian Examiner* 44 (1852): 471.

41 West, Earl Irvin. "John Quincy Adams: Legacy of a Puritan" in "Religion and Politics in the Jacksonian Era." Ph.D. dissertation. Indiana University, 1968. pp. 29-59.

CHESTER ARTHUR

This obscure, accidental president seems to have had little interest in religion, despite the fact that he was a Baptist minister's son. Indeed, there is no definitive biography of him and almost no interest in his Presidency.

His wife was an Episcopalian and he attended St. John's Church on Lafayette Square near the White House. (She died shortly before he became Vice President.) Apparently, he never formally joined any church.

Vernon Hampton's chapter on Arthur is the best summation of his religious interests.

See Bonnell, item 3, pp. 142-144.

See Fuller, item 8, pp. 146-147.

See Hampton, V., item 10, pp. 71-82.

See Hampton, W., item 11, pp. 67-70.

See Isely, item 12, pp. 163-168.

JAMES BUCHANAN

Like many 19th-century public figures, James Buchanan received a strong religious upbringing, drifted away from religious practice during a lifetime of public service, and then united with a church in the closing years of his life.

Raised in the Presbyterian tradition, Buchanan had a lifelong serious interest in religion, but had a difficult time accepting its traditional doctrines. Always a tolerant man, he respected other religions. After he left the White House, he united formally with the Presbyterian Church--after a nasty hassle. It seems that the fanatical abolitionists had taken control of the Northern branch and refused to admit Buchanan because of his conciliatory policies toward the South on the eve of the Civil War.

Both Hensel and Klein are indispensable sources for a study of Buchanan's faith.

See Bonnell, item 3, pp. 102-106.

See Fuller, item 8, pp. 96-100.

See Hampton, V., item 10, pp. 222-231.

See Hampton, W., item 11, pp. 47-50.

See Isely, item 12, pp. 115-120.

42 Hensel, William U. A Pennsylvania Presbyterian President. Philadelphia: Presbyterian Social Union, 1907.

43 ------. The Religious Character and Convictions of James Buchanan. Lancaster: Intelligencer Print, 1912.

44 Klein, Philip S. "James Buchanan: Selfish Politician or Christian Statesman?" Journal of Presbyterian History 42 (March 1964): 1-18.

15

JIMMY CARTER

As Paul Boller, Jr. suggested (see item 2), Jimmy Carter was one of four or five very committed evangelicals to serve as U.S. President. His religious convictions apparently were well-developed and highly influential in his personal life but were disturbing to enough voters to provide controversy during the 1976 campaign. Much of the material cited in this bibliography is of the impressionistic/journalistic mode.

Wesley Pippert's compilation of President Carter's Sunday School class at Washington's First Baptist Church (The Spiritual Journey of Jimmy Carter) is perhaps the best place to begin a study of Carter's complex religious identity. Pippert was a White House reporter who became a close friend and interpreter of Carter. James Baker's A Southern Baptist in the White House is an insightful analysis from the pen of a professor of history who writes from a liberal Baptist perspective. Professor Ronald Flowers of Texas Christian University gives an excellent overview of the Carter Presidency in his Journal of Church and State article.

The Nielsen book is rather shallow and flawed, especially its chapters on Carter's relationship with the Catholic and Jewish communities. Howard Norton and Bob Slosser's The Miracle of Jimmy Carter was a campaign tract penned by two evangelicals who thought Carter would be some kind of Saviour-Messiah figure who would restore evangelical political power. (When Carter failed to do so, co-author Slosser transferred his affections to Ronald Reagan and wrote a ghastly book promoting Reagan's reelection.) The books by Jessica Gaver and James Hefley are worthless attempts to propagandize for the Southern Baptists by cashing in on the Carter phenomenon. The article by Don Winter, exploring Carter's dependence on Reinhold Niebuhr's thought, is illuminating. For highly sympathetic evaluations of Carter's religious views, see the articles by Christian Century editor James Wall.

45 Abram, Morris B. "Governor Carter's Religion." Nation 223 (September 25, 1976): 261-262.

46 Baker, James T. "Jimmy Carter's Religion." Commonweal 103 (July 2, 1976): 430-433.

47 ------. A Southern Baptist in the White House. Philadelphia: The Westminster Press, 1977.

48 Briggs, Kenneth A. "The Gospel According to Peanuts." Christian Century 93 (May 12, 1976): 452-454.

49 "Carter and the Bishops." Commonweal 103 (September 24, 1976): 611-612.

50 "Carter and the God Issue." Newsweek 87 (April 5, 1976): 18-19.

51 Carter, Jimmy and Wesley G. Pippert. "My Personal Faith in God." Christianity Today 27 (March 4, 1977): 14.

52 "Carter the Deacon." Time 107 (April 12, 1976): 14.

53 "Carter's Church." Newsweek 92 (August 28, 1978): 11.

54 Castelli, Jim. "How Catholics Voted." Commonweal 103 (December 3, 1976): 780-782.

55 "Cruelty of Morality: Abortion Views of Jimmy Carter." Nation 225 (July 23, 1977): 68-69.

56 "Do Presidential Rights to Privacy Include Religion?" Christianity Today 23 (September 21, 1979): 12.

57 Douglas, Bruce. "The Gamble of Carter's Piety." Christianity and Crisis 36 (October 4, 1976): 220-224.

58 Drinan, Robert F. "Governor Carter's Commitment to Christian Concerns." America 135 (October 30, 1976): 270-272.

59 Erickson, Keith V. "Jimmy Carter, The Rhetoric of Private and Civic Piety." Western Journal of Speech Communication 44 (1980): 221-235.

60 Flowers, Ronald B. "President Jimmy Carter, Evangelicalism, Church-State Relations and Civil Religion."

Journal of Church and State 25 (Winter 1983): 113-132.

61 Freese, A.S. "Carter's Religious Upbringing." Modern Maturity 20 (February 1977): 31.

62 Gaver, Jessica Russell. The Faith of Jimmy Carter. New York: Manor Books, 1977.

63 "Georgia Deacon's Day." Time (August 2, 1976): 16.

64 Hefley, James and Marti. The Church That Produced a President. New York: Wyden, 1977.

65 Himmelfarb, Milton. "Carter and the Jews." Commentary 62 (August 1976): 45-48.

66 Hughes, Arthur J. "Amazin' Jimmy and a Mighty Fortress Was Our Teddy: Theodore Roosevelt and Jimmy Carter, The Religious Link." Presidential Studies Quarterly 9 (1979): 80-83.

67 Hutcheson, R.G. "Jimmy Carter's Moral Presidency." Christian Century 96 (November 21, 1979): 1155-1156.

68 "Jimmy, the Bible and Brezhnev." Time 110 (August 1, 1977): 12-13.

69 Jorstad, Erling. Evangelicals in the White House. New York: Edwin Mellen Press, 1981.

70 King, N. "Carter and the Church." National Review 29 (April 1, 1977): 384-385.

71 Lipset, Seymour M. "Catholic Defection." New Republic 175 (October 2, 1976): 10-11.

72 Maddox, Robert L. Preacher at the White House. Nashville: Broadman Press, 1984.

73 "Mandate of Heaven: Carter Administration's Religious Side." Christian Century 94 (January 1977): 29.

74 Mathews, A.H. "Crusade for the White House: Skirmishes in a Holy War." Christianity Today 21 (November 19, 1976): 48-51.

75 Menendez, Albert J. "The Religious Issue Revisited." Humanist 36 (July 1976): 38-40.

76 ------. "Will Evangelicals Swing the Election?" Christianity Today 20 (June 18, 1976): 32-33.

77 Miller, William Lee. "Defending Carter's Heresies." New Republic 175 (October 9, 1976): 17-19.

78 Moore, Arthur. "Piety on the Potomac Revisited." Christianity and Crisis 39 (August 20, 1979): 196-197.

79 Murphy, K. "Not Since Jefferson and Madison." Saturday Review 3 (September 4, 1976): 8-11.

80 Nannes, Caspar. "New Teacher, Pupil at Sunday School." Christianity Today 21 (April 1, 1977): 52-53.

81 Nielsen, Niels. The Religion of President Carter. Nashville: Thomas Nelson, 1977.

82 Norton, Howard and Bob Slosser. The Miracle of Jimmy Carter. Plainfield: Logos, 1976.

83 Osborn, John. "Carter and God." New Republic 180 (June 16, 1979): 9-11.

84 Pippert, Wesley G. "Carter at Sunday School." Christian Century 94 (May 11, 1977): 446.

85 ------. "Does Carter's Christianity Count?" Christianity Today 23 (November 3, 1978): 15.

86 ------, ed. The Spiritual Journey of Jimmy Carter. New York: Macmillan, 1979.

87 Plowman, Edward E. "Carter's Presence Confirms Clout of Evangelical Broadcasters." Christianity Today 24 (February 22, 1980): 48-49.

88 ------. "Democrats: God in the Garden." Christianity Today 20 (August 6, 1976): 34-36.

89 ------. "New Church Member in Town." Christianity Today 21 (February 18, 1977): 54-55.

90 Randall, Claire. "Carter at Camp David: An Experience of Renewal." Christian Century 96 (August 1, 1979): 750-751.

91 Reed, W.A. "Jimmy Carter: Salesman for God." *Good Housekeeping* 186 (May 1978): 158-159.

92 Reeves, Richard. "Is Jimmy Carter Good for the Jews?" *New York* 11 (May 24, 1976): 22-24.

93 Richmond, M.E.M. "Carter and the Jews." *Christian Century* 93 (October 27, 1976): 926-928.

94 Stapleton, Ruth Carter. "President's Evangelist Sister Talks About the Jimmy I Know." Interview in *U.S. News* 85 (September 18, 1978): 24-26.

95 Wall, James M. "Carter and the Religious Factor." *Christian Century* 94 (August 31, 1977): 739-740.

96 ------. "When Religious Prejudice Dulls Judgment." *Christian Century* 96 (August 29, 1979): 811-812.

97 ------. "Words of Faith From Jimmy Carter." *Christian Century* 96 (January 17, 1979): 38-39.

98 Winter, Don. "The Carter-Niebuhr Connection." *National Journal* 10 (February 4, 1978): 188-192.

99 "With Carter in Church." *Christianity Today* 22 (September 8, 1978): 56.

GROVER CLEVELAND

Grover Cleveland is an anomaly: a Presbyterian minister's son who seemed to have minimal interest in religion. He remained a nominal Presbyterian all his life but seems to have had no strong religious interests or connections. Nor were there any major church-state disputes during his two terms. Hence, there is limited information about him.

See Bonnell, item 3, pp. 146-150.

See Fuller, item 8, pp. 148-152.

See Hampton, V., item 10, pp. 83-90; pp. 379-380.

See Hampton, W., item 11, pp. 71-72.

See Isely, item 12, pp. 171-176.

CALVIN COOLIDGE

This taciturn New Englander was a lifelong Congregationalist who went to church faithfully. But he seems to have had no intellectual curiosity about religion. He saw religion as an exclusively personal matter and disliked clergy who discussed politics or the social gospel. Still, he inaugurated such customs as the President's Christmas Message to the nation and the lighting of the national Christmas tree.

The Republican-leaning Literary Digest followed Coolidge's religion avidly, remaining the best source, along with Bliss Isely, for the subject.

See Bonnell, item 3, pp. 194-198.

See Fuller, item 8, pp. 190-194.

See Hampton, V., item 10, pp. 265-279; pp. 369-374.

See Hampton, W., item 11, pp. 101-106.

See Isely, item 12, pp. 227-232.

100 "The President on the Bible." Literary Digest 93 (May 7, 1927): 32.

101 "President's Sermon to the Nation." Literary Digest 87 (November 7, 1925): 29.

102 "Religious Beliefs of the Next President." Literary Digest 78 (August 11, 1923): 7-9.

103 Sneed, J. Richard. "Calvin Coolidge's Religion." Literary Digest 105 (February 4, 1933): 20.

DWIGHT EISENHOWER

Dwight Eisenhower's religious profile is one of the more unusual, perhaps because as a military leader for nearly forty years, he rarely, if ever, attended church, despite a strict upbringing by parents originally associated with the River Brethren sect. (Later they became Jehovah's Witnesses.)

But, as President, he joined the Presbyterian Church by Baptism the Sunday after his inauguration, composed a prayer for the inaugural ceremonies, frequently pontificated on religious values, attempted to make the National Day of Prayer a major ceremony, signed the act adding "In God We Trust" to the Pledge of Allegiance, began cabinet meetings with prayer, and established the Presidential Prayer Breakfast. His critics called his eight-year reign an unctuous period of "piety on the Potomac," but many evangelical and Catholic admirers hailed his staunch public advocacy of religion as the prescription to society's ills and a guarantee of democracy's survival.

Many of Eisenhower's own religious statements are noted in this bibliography and should be studied by students of the period. Paul Hutchinson's overview in <u>Christian Century</u> is probably the best summary of Ike's personal religious journey. Washington journalist Caspar Nannes shows a president completely at home with his church in a factual, anecdotal article.

William Lee Miller, Robert Fitch, Ernest Lefever and Senator Matthew Neely were critical of Eisenhower's public professions of national faith, seeing it as partisan manifestations or innocuous civil religion.

See Bonnell, item 3, pp. 218-223.

See Fuller, item 8, pp. 212-218.

See Isely, item 12, pp. 259-266.

104 "Address by President Eisenhower Given at the National Conference of Catholic Charities. New York, September 26, 1960." Catholic Charities Review 44 (October 1960): 5+.

105 Agar, Herbert. "Prayer for the New President." Saturday Review 36 (January 17, 1953): 7-8+.

106 "A Changing Symbol: Proposed Visit of President Eisenhower to the Shinto Meiji Shrine in Tokyo." Commonweal 72 (June 10, 1960): 270.

107 "Does the President Know the Church?" Ave Maria 79 (April 10, 1954): 4.

108 "Eisenhower at Assembly of World Council." Christian Century 71 (September 1, 1954): 1048.

109 Eisenhower, Dwight D. "Logistics of Faith." Address, August 19, 1954. Vital Speeches 20 (September 1, 1954): 702-704.

110 ------. "Religious and Civil Liberty." Excerpt from remarks at Interchurch Center, N.Y. Christian Century 75 (October 22, 1958): 1195.

111 ------. "Ike on Religion." Excerpts from news conference September 7, 1960. U.S. News 49 (September 19, 1960): 90.

112 ------. "Prayer in 2nd Inaugural Address." National Parent Teacher 51 (March 1957): 2-3.

113 ------. "Uniting the World Through Religion and Education." Remarks September 9, 1959. U.S. Dept of State Bulletin 41 (September 28, 1959): 447-448.

114 "Faith of the Candidates." Time 60 (September 22, 1952): 55.

115 "Faith in High Places." Newsweek 48 (September 24, 1956): 98-100.

116 Fitch, Robert E. "Piety and Politics in Eisenhower." Antioch Review 15 (Summer 1955): 148-154.

117 "Great Moral Crusade." Address, July 25, 1954. Vital Speeches 20 (August 15, 1954): 642-643.

118 Gustafson, Merlin. "Religion of a President." Christian Century 86 (April 30, 1969): 610-613.

119 Hartnett, Robert C. "Religious Views of Candidates." America 87 (September 27, 1952): 616-617.

120 Hutchinson, Paul. "The President's Religious Faith." Christian Century 121 (March 24, 1954): 362-369.

121 "Ike's Faith." Time 60 (August 18, 1952): 12-14.

122 "Ike's Faith." Time 61 (April 13, 1953): 91.

123 Lefever, Ernest W. "The Candidates' Religious Views." Christian Century 73 (September 19, 1956): 1072-1075.

124 Miller, William Lee. Piety Along the Potomac. Boston: Houghton Mifflin, 1964.

125 ------. "Religion, Politics and the Great Crusade." Reporter 9 (July 7, 1953): 14-16.

126 ------. "The Religious Revival and American Politics." Confluence 4 (1955): 44-50.

127 Nadich, Judah. Eisenhower and the Jews. New York: Twayne, 1953.

128 Nannes, Caspar. "The President and His Pastor." Colliers 136 (November 11, 1955): 29-31.

129 Neely, Matthew. "The President and His Church." U.S. News 38 (April 8, 1955): 50-52.

130 O'Brien, John C. "Prayerful President." Sign 33 (August 1953): 19-21.

131 Parmlew, Helen. "Graham Recalls His Influence on Eisenhower's Religion." Religious News Service (April 12, 1985).

132 Plowman, Edward E. "Ike's Faith." Christianity Today 13 (April 15, 1969): 33.

133 "Prayer and Preparation." Time 61 (January 26, 1953): 18.

134 "Prayer at Cabinet Meetings." *America* 88 (March 7, 1953): 612.

135 "President Attends Red Mass." *America* 90 (February 13, 1954): 493.

136 "President Prays." *America* 92 (October 9, 1954): 29-30.

137 "President Stakes Down His Faith." *Christian Century* 70 (February 11, 1953): 155.

138 "President's Prayer." *Ave Maria* 77 (February 7, 1953): 162.

139 "President's Prayer." *Family Digest* 9 (July 1954): 24.

140 "President's Prayer." *Nation* 176 (January 31, 1953): 91.

141 Entry omitted.

142 "Religion, a Dominant Theme." *U.S. News* 34 (February 13, 1953): 4.

143 "Religion in the Campaign." *Commonweal* 65 (October 12, 1956): 35.

144 "Senator Neely's Speech on Eisenhower's Religious Conviction." *Commonweal* 62 (April 15, 1955): 33.

145 "Sermon and Parade." *Christian Century* 74 (February 6, 1957): 158-159.

146 Weil, Eric. "Religion and Politics." *Confluence* 4 (July 1955): 202-206.

MILLARD FILLMORE

Millard Fillmore remains, justifiably, an obscure president. He seems to have been a Unitarian in religion, though he had no strong religious interests. Apparently, he withdrew from the Unitarians because of their intense criticism of his record as president on the subject of slavery. (Buchanan, Pierce and Andrew Johnson also suffered at the hands of Northern Protestant abolitionists.)

He seems to have played fast and loose with denominations. His first wife was a Baptist minister's daughter but their marriage was solemnized in an Episcopal Church. His second wife was a Baptist. His funeral service was officiated by Baptist, Episcopalian and Presbyterian clergy--but no Unitarian was present, though Fillmore had been a charter member of the first Unitarian Society in Buffalo.

See Bonnell, item 3, pp. 92-94.

See Fuller, item 8, pp. 89-91.

See Hampton, V., item 10, pp. 220-222.

See Hampton, W., item 11, p. 44.

See Isely, item 12, pp. 99-104.

GERALD FORD

Our 38th President was a lifelong Episcopalian who seems to have developed evangelical tendencies in his later years. His religion was of the quiet, undemonstrative variety. While faithfully attending Episcopal churches, he had a close relationship with an evangelist named Billy Zeoli.

The best source for Ford's religion is a chapter in a book on evangelicals in Washington by veteran journalist Edward Plowman and free-lance writer James Hefley.

147 Doyle, Barrie and James C. Hefley. "Prayer and a Quiet Faith." Christianity Today 18 (August 30, 1974): 33.

148 Hefley, James C. and Edward E. Plowman. "Ford's Faith" in Washington: Christians in the Corridors of Power. Wheaton: Tyndale House, 1975. pp. 13-36.

149 Plowman, Edward E. "Ford's First Month: Christ and Conflict." Christianity Today 18 (September 27, 1974): 39.

150 Spoelstra, Watson. "Sunday Brunch at Jerry's Place." Christianity Today 20 (March 1976): 48.

151 Zeoli, Billy. "President Ford's Personal Prayers." Ladies Home Journal 92 (December 1975): 67.

JAMES GARFIELD

Garfield was our only "preacher President," though he was a lay preacher, not a formally ordained pastor, in the Disciples of Christ. Because of his personal piety and rectitude, Garfield was a favorite of 19th-century evangelicals and still comes off as saintly and noble in Vernon Hampton's book, which treats Garfield rather thoroughly.

His tragic assassination, especially the prolonged nature of his suffering, added to his martyr image. He was a zealous evangelical preacher and a noted educator but his Presidency is not marked by any major achievements. In common with many evangelicals of his era, he indulged in a good deal of anti-Catholicism to win elections. (See article by John Gilmary Shea.)

The book and doctoral dissertation by Woodrow Wasson are the most thorough sources for Garfield's religion. The Rushford dissertation is also recommended.

See Bonnell, item 3, pp. 136-139.

See Fuller, item 8, pp. 139-145.

See Hampton, V., item 10, pp. 58-71.

See Hampton, W., item 11, pp. 65-66.

See Isely, item 12, pp. 155-160.

152 Banks, Louis Albert. The Religious Life of Famous Americans. New York: American Tract Society, 1904. pp. 53-62.

153 Rushford, Jerry Bryant. "Political Disciple: The Relationship between James A. Garfield and the Disciples of Christ." Ph.D. dissertation. University of California, Santa Barbara, 1977.

154 Shea, John Gilmary. "The Anti-Catholic Issue in the Late Election—The Relation of Catholics to Political Parties." *American Catholic Quarterly Review* 6 (1881): 36-50.

155 Steiner, Franklin. *The Religious Beliefs of Our Presidents*. Girard, Ks.: Haldeman-Julius, 1936. pp. 146-149.

156 Sunderland, Byron. *The Problem of Prayer and the Death of President Garfield*. Washington, D.C.: E. Henkle, 1881.

157 Wasson, Woodrow W. *James A. Garfield: His Religion and Education. A Study in the Religious and Educational Thought and Activity of an American Statesman.* Nashvile: Tennessee Book Co., 1952.

158 ------. "James A. Garfield and Religion: A Study in the Religious Thought and Activity of an American Statesman." Ph.D. dissertation. University of California, 1948.

ULYSSES S. GRANT

Ulysses S. Grant's life was almost totally devoid of formal religious activity, though his wife and parents were Methodists and he attended church with them. His lengthy two-volume autobiography, Personal Memoirs, contains not one line about religion.

His family, however, terrified that he would die unbaptized, brought in a certain Reverend J. P. Newman to attend the dying former President in 1885. Newman concocted a fanciful tale that Grant had been converted and baptized hours before his death. Close friends, including Mark Twain, exposed the hoax. (Grant had refused baptism and had been near a coma when death came.)

Still, as President, Grant issued ritualistic statements commending the Bible. He also blasted the Catholic Church over the issue of public aid for church schools and issued an infamous anti-Semitic order during his days as Union Army general.

See Bonnell, item 3, pp. 122-127.

See Fuller, Item 8, pp. 125-131.

See Hampton, V., item 10, pp. 241-245; pp. 353-354.

See Hampton, W., item 11, pp. 61-62.

See Isely, item 12, pp. 139-144

159 Keller, Robert H., Jr. "The Protestant Churches and Grant's Peace Policy: A Study in Church-State Relations, 1869-1882." Ph.D. dissertation. University of Chicago, 1967.

WARREN G. HARDING

Warren Harding may have been our most irreligious president, even if nominally a Baptist. His personal life was a scandal; his Presidency, a disgrace. He did attend church occasionally to please his wife, but there is no evidence that he paid the slightest attention to religious duties or values.

The best source, such as it is, for information on Harding's religion can be found in the William Hampton volume, though Hampton's interpretations are dubious at best.

See Bonnell, item 3, pp. 188-192.

See Fuller, item 8, pp. 184-189.

See Hampton, V., item 10, pp. 264-265; pp. 368-369.

See Hampton W., item 11, pp. 91-100.

See Isely, item 12, pp. 219-224.

BENJAMIN HARRISON

Harrison was a convinced evangelical Presbyterian whose social life revolved around the church, which he served as elder and deacon. He was austere in a Calvinist way, frowning on entertainments and levity.

His Presidency was serious and sober and he tended to continue the anti-Catholic policies of Republican presidents since Grant.

Always a staunch churchman, he was several times a delegate to the General Assembly of the Presbyterian Church where, somewhat surprisingly, he supported progressive policies.

See Bonnell, item 3, pp. 152-155.

See Fuller, item 8, pp. 153-156.

See Hampton, V., item 10, pp. 248-250; pp. 341-343.

See Hampton, W., item 11, pp. 73-75.

See Isely, item 12, pp. 179-184.

160 Banks, Louis Albert. The Religious Life of Famous Americans. New York: American Tract Society, 1904. pp. 237-245.

161 Sievers, Harry J. "The Catholic Indian School Issue and the Presidential Election of 1892." Catholic Historical Review 38 (July 1952): 129-155.

WILLIAM HENRY HARRISON

About William Henry Harrison's religion little is known. He was a Virginia Episcopalian who had been baptized but may not have been confirmed. He apparently read the Bible and kept the Sabbath. The rector of St. John's Church in Washington told mourners at Harrison's funeral that the President had expressed a desire to enter into full communion on Easter Sunday--one week away. Harrison served only one month as President, dying of pneumonia contracted at his inauguration.

See Bonnell, item 3, pp. 68-71.

See Fuller, item 8, pp. 73-76.

See Hampton, V., item 10, p. 214.

See Hampton, W., item 11, p. 35.

See Isely, item 12, pp. 67-72.

RUTHERFORD HAYES

Hayes found religion intellectually absorbing. He spent a great deal of his life wrestling with religious and ethical questions, but he never joined any church. His wife, "Lemonade Lucy," was an avid Methodist and Prohibitionist, and Hayes accompanied her faithfully to services at Foundry Methodist Church in the nation's capital.

Hayes was intensely interested in the literary aspects of the Bible. He claimed to be unable to comprehend the statements of many of the historic creeds of the church. He saw churchgoing as a civilizing act.

But he called himself a Christian on numerous occasions. And his White House was a model of evangelical virtue, complete with daily prayers, Bible reading and Sunday night hymn-singing sessions.

Fuller and Green are the best sources for Hayes' religion.

See Bonnell, item 3, pp. 130-133.

See Fuller, item 8, pp. 132-138.

See Hampton, V., item 10, pp. 245-248; pp. 376-379.

See Hampton, W., item 11, pp. 63-64.

See Isely, item 12, pp. 147-152.

HERBERT HOOVER

The "Quaker Engineer" was a serious adherent of his childhood faith. His mother, in fact, was a Quaker "preacher" as Quakers understand that term. Hoover viewed religion as ethical humanitarianism and was able to reconcile science and religious faith.

His wife was originally an Episcopalian who became a Quaker. They were married by a Catholic priest, an old family friend, in an unusual ceremony that required a dispensation from the bishop.

Vernon Hampton's Religious Background of the White House is the best overall summary for Hoover's faith. Gustafson looks at Hoover's record on church-state issues. Gustafson notes that Hoover appointed almost no Catholics or Jews to any administrative post but did appoint some noted anti-Catholic agitators. The National Catholic Welfare Conference even issued a public protest of Hoover's appointment policies in 1930.

The articles by Richelsen and Wilson are also useful.

For additional material on the Hoover-Smith campaign see Albert J. Menendez, Religious Conflict in America (New York: Garland Publishing, 1985): 57-60.

See Bonnell, item 3, pp. 200-203.

See Fuller, item 8, pp. 195-200.

See Hampton, V., item 10, pp. 101-119.

See Isely, item 12, pp. 235-240.

162 Chesterton, G.K. "Luther and Mr. Hoover." America 44 (November 29, 1930): 176-177.

163 Gummere, W. "Quakers and Catholics: Two Horns of One Dilemma." *Atlantic Monthly* 142 (September 1928): 428-430.

164 Gustafson, Merlin. "President Hoover and the National Religion." *Journal of Church and State* 16 (Winter 1974): 85-100.

165 "Herbert Hoover as a Quaker." *Nation* 127 (October 17, 1928): 388.

166 Hinshaw, David. *Herbert Hoover: American Quaker.* New York: Farrar, Straus and Co., 1950.

167 "Hoover and the Religious Issue." *Independent* 121 (October 13, 1928): 341.

168 Mather, P.B. "Quaker Requiem." *Christian Century* 81 (November 18, 1964): 1446.

169 Moley, Ray. "Hoover, the Great Quaker." *Newsweek* 35 (April 10, 1950): 88.

170 Parsons, Wilfrid. "The Pope, the President and the Governor." *America* 47 (September 3, 1932): 517-519.

171 "Pope and President on Economics." *America* 45 (June 27, 1931): 269.

172 Richelsen, John. "Herbert Hoover and the Quakers." *Current History* 30 (April 1929): 79-83.

173 Wilson, John R.M. "The Quaker and the Sword: Herbert Hoover's Relations with the Military." *Military Affairs* 38 (April 1974): 41-47.

ANDREW JACKSON

Andrew Jackson's religious life was as complex and varied as his secular affairs. Raised with great respect for Christianity and the Bible, Jackson was too busy with his military and political career to devote time or energy to religion until later in life.

As President, he was a strong supporter of separation of church and state and religious tolerance. He refused to proclaim a day of fasting and prayer, believing that Americans did not need government telling them when to worship. He appointed Catholics to his cabinet and to the U.S. Supreme Court.

His wife, Rachel, was a devout Presbyterian, and he had long planned to join the church. He steadfastly refused to do so while President lest his action be misconstrued as a political stunt. He built Rachel a church on the grounds of his estate in Nashville and faithfully attended church after her death. He joined the local Presbyterian church after leaving the White House.

The chapter in West's doctoral dissertation is unfailingly illuminating. Walker and Stickley are also excellent.

See Bonnell, item 3, pp. 56-60.

See Fuller, item 8, pp. 60-67.

See Hampton, V., item 10, pp. 343-44.

See Hampton, W., item 11, pp. 31-33.

See Isely, item 12, pp. 51-56.

174 Banks, Louis Albert. The Religious Life of Famous Americans. New York: American Tract Society, 1904. pp. 175-184.

175 Dahl, Curtis. "The Clergyman, the Hussy and Old Hickory; Ezra Stiles Ely and the Peggy Eaton Affair." Journal of Presbyterian History 52 (Summer 1974): 137-155.

176 Horn, Stanley F. The Hermitage. New York: Greenberg, 1950. pp. 187-206.

177 Langley, Lester D. "Jacksonian America and the Ottoman Empire." Muslim World 68 (January 1978): 46-56.

178 Steiner, B.C. "Jackson and the Missionaries." American History Review 29 (July 1924): 722-723.

179 Stickley, Julia Ward. "Catholic Ceremonies in the White House, 1832-1833." Catholic Historical Review 51 (July 1965): 192-198.

180 Walker, Arda. "The Religious Views of Andrew Jackson." East Tennessee Historical Society Publication No. 17 (1945): 61-70.

181 West, Earl Irvin. "Andrew Jackson: Religion's Enigmatic Advocate" in "Religion and Politics in the Jacksonian Era." Ph.D. dissertation. Indiana University, 1968. pp. 158-191.

THOMAS JEFFERSON

Jefferson's religion has long intrigued scholars. Perhaps that interest is due, in part, to our third President's interest in religious issues. He was, after all, our only President to rewrite the New Testament in his spare time. Jefferson's attempt to demythologize the record, denuding it of all supernatural occurrences, made him a controversial figure within his own lifetime.

But was he a freethinker, a skeptic, an agnostic, a Unitarian, or an Episcopalian? One must read the literature to make an informed judgment. Sanford and Foote are the best overall studies. Sanford is thorough if dry, while Foote gives a Unitarian interpretation. Some authors, including Brydon, Hall, Horsley, Kinsolving, and Stowe, place Jefferson within the Episcopalian orbit.

Jefferson's Bible and his views of the Bible in general, are explored by Adams, Adler, Brown, Goodspeed, Fesperman, Hardon, and Mabee. His views on religious education are studied by Costanzo, Healey, and Locigno. The origins of his anti-clericalism are explored by Luebke.

Good overviews of Jefferson's religious life are found in Gould, Knoles, and Wicks, while the context within which he developed intellectually is handled well by Buckley and Kay. His relationship with the Baptists is depicted in Christian and Paschall.

Jefferson's preeminent contribution may have been his advocacy of religious freedom and separation of church and state. See Crawford, Foote, Forrest, Kuper, Little, Mead, Plochl and Trainor for some thoughtful and insightful observations.

An interesting debate over Jefferson's alleged dependence on Cardinal Bellarmine in the development of his libertarian ideals can be seen by comparing Catholic historian Gaillard Hunt and Protestant historian David Schaff.

Two interesting Catholic views of Jefferson can be seen in Rager and Zwierlein.

See Bonnell, item 3, pp. 32-36.

See Fuller, item 8, pp. 28-38.

See Hampton, V., item 10, pp. 383-385.

See Hampton, W., item 11, pp. 21-23.

See Isely, item 12, pp. 19-24.

182 Adams, Dickinson Ward. "Jefferson's Politics of Morality: The Purpose and Meaning of His Extracts from the Evangelists," "The Philosophy of Jesus of Nazareth" and "The Life and Morals of Jesus of Nazareth." Ph.D. dissertation. Brown University, 1970.

183 Adler, Cyrus. "Jefferson Bible." Cosmopolitan 38 (1905): 340-344.

184 Anderson, John R. "A Twentieth-Century Reflection of the American Enlightenment." Social Education 29 (1965): 159-163.

185 Bauer, Gerald. "The Quest for Religious Freedom in Virginia." Historical Magazine of the Protestant Episcopal Church 41 (1972): 83-93.

186 Bennett, H. Omer. "The Religion of Thomas Jefferson." Social Science 5 (1930): 460-465.

187 Brent, Robert A. "The Jeffersonian Outlook on Religion." Southern Quarterly 5 (1967): 417-432.

188 Brown, Barbara. "Jefferson Bible: Compilation of the Words of Jesus." Mentor 17 (July 1929): 57-59.

189 Brydon, G. Maclaren. "Thomas Jefferson-The Churchman." Tyler's Quarterly 25 (1943): 73-75.

190 Buckley, Thomas E. Church and State in Revolutionary Virginia 1776-1787. Charlottesville: University of Virginia Press, 1977.

191 Christian, John T. "The Religion of Thomas Jefferson." Review and Expositor 16 (1919): 295-307.

192 Costanzo, Joseph F. "Thomas Jefferson, Religious Education and Public Law." Journal of Public Law 8 (1961): 81-108.

193 Cousins, Norman, ed. 'In God We Trust,' The Religious Beliefs and Ideas of the American Founding Fathers. New York: Harper, 1958. pp. 114-216.

194 Crawford, Nelson Antrim. "Thomas Jefferson and Religious Freedom." American Collector 2 (1926): 292-295.

195 Crothers, Samuel McCord. The Religion of Thomas Jefferson, Author of the Declaration of Independence. Boston: American Unitarian Association, 1926.

196 Davis, Thurston N. and R. Freeman Butts. "Footnote on Church-State; 'Say Nothing of My Religion.'" School and Society 81 (1955): 180-187.

197 Drouin, Edmond G. "Madison and Jefferson on Clergy in the Legislature." America 138 (1978): 58-59.

198 Eliot, Frederick May. "What Kind of Christian Was Thomas Jefferson?" in Frederick May Eliot: An Anthology, ed. Alfred P. Stiernotte. Boston: Beacon Press, 1959.

199 Ericson, Edward L. "Freethinker in the White House" in The Free Mind Through the Ages. New York: Frederick Ungar, 1985. pp. 105-120.

200 Fesperman, Francis I. "Jefferson's Bible." Ohio Journal of Religious Studies 4 (October 1976): 78-88.

201 Foote, Henry Wilder. Thomas Jefferson: Champion of Religious Freedom, Advocate of Christian Morals. Boston: Beacon Press, 1947.

202 Forrest, W.M. "Thomas Jefferson and Religious Freedom." Virginia Journal of Education 19 (1926): 355-357.

203 Fritchman, Stephen Hole. "Thomas Jefferson" in Men of Liberty: Ten Unitarian Pioneers. Boston: Beacon Press, 1944.

204 Goodspeed, Edgar J. "Thomas Jefferson and the Bible." *Harvard Theological Review* 40 (1947): 71-76.

205 Gould, William Drum. "The Religious Opinions of Thomas Jefferson." Ph.D. dissertation. Boston University, 1929.

206 ------. "The Religious Opinions of Thomas Jefferson." *Missouri Valley Historical Review* 20 (1933): 191-208.

207 Hall, J. Leslie. "The Religious Opinions of Thomas Jefferson." *Sewanee Review* 21 (1913): 164-176.

208 Halliday, E.M. "Nature's God and the Founding Fathers." *American Heritage* 14 (October 1963): 4-7, 100-106.

209 Hamilton, J.G. deRoulhac. "Jefferson and Religion." *Reviewer* 5 (October 1925): 5-15.

210 Hardon, John A. "The Jefferson Bible." *American-Ecclesiastical Review* 130 (1954): 361-375.

211 Healey, Robert M. *Jefferson on Religion in Public Education.* New Haven: Yale University Press, 1962.

212 Horsley, Catherine Dunscombe. "Jefferson—The Churchman." *Tyler's Quarterly* 25 (1943): 1-2.

213 Hunt, Gaillard. "The Virginia Declaration of Rights and Cardinal Bellarmine." *Catholic Historical Review* 3 (1917): 276-289.

214 Huntley, William B. "Jefferson's Public and Private Religion." *South Atlantic Quarterly* 79 (1980): 286-301.

215 Hutchins, Robert Maynard. "Thomas Jefferson and the Intellectual Love of God" in *No Friendly Voice.* Chicago: University of Chicago Press, 1936.

216 Jefferson, Thomas. *Republican Notes on Religion and an Act to Establish Religious Freedom.* Danbury, Ct.: Thomas Rowe, 1803.

217 "Jefferson and the Ketoctin Baptist Association." *Bulletin of the Loudoun County Historical Society* 1 (1958): 56-60.

218 Jones, Edgar DeWitt. "Thomas Jefferson and Religion." Christian Century 43 (1926): 774-775.

219 Kay, Miryan Neulander. "Separation of Church and State in Jeffersonian Virginia." Ph.D. dissertation. University of Kentucky, 1967.

220 Kilgo, John Carlisle. "A Study of Thomas Jefferson's Religious Belief." Trinity Archive 13 (March 1900): 331-346.

221 Kinsolving, Arthur B. "The Religious Opinions of Thomas Jefferson." Historical Magazine of the Protestant Episcopal Church 20 (1951): 325-327.

222 Knoles, George Harmon. "The Religious Ideas of Thomas Jefferson." Missouri Valley Historical Review 30 (1943): 187-204.

223 Kuper, Theodore Fred. "Thomas Jefferson, Champion of Religious Freedom." The Courier 2 (February 1936): 9-10, 20.

224 Little, David. "Thomas Jefferson's Religious Views and Their Influence on the Supreme Court's Interpretation of the First Amendment." Catholic University Law Review 26 (1976): 57-72.

225 ------. "The Origins of Perplexity: Civil Religion and Moral Belief in the Thought of Thomas Jefferson" in American Civil Religion, ed. Russell E. Richey and Donald G. Jones. New York: Harper and Row, 1974.

226 Locigno, J.P. "Jefferson on Church and State in Education." Religious Education 64 (May 1969): 172-175.

227 Luebke, Fred C. "The Development of Thomas Jefferson's Religious Opinions, 1743-1800." M.A. thesis. Claremont Graduate School, 1958.

228 ------. "The Origins of Thomas Jefferson's Anti-Clericalism." Church History 32 (1963): 344-356.

229 Mabee, Charles. "Thomas Jefferson's Anti-Clerical Bible." Historical Magazine of the Protestant Episcopal Church 48 (1979): 473-481.

230 Mead, Sidney Earl. "Thomas Jefferson's 'Fair Experiment'-Religious Freedom." Religion in Life 23 (1954): 566-579.

231 Mehta, M.J. "The Religion of Thomas Jefferson." Indo-Asian Culture 16 (1967): 96-103.

232 Mott, Royden J. "Sources of Jefferson's Ecclesiastical Views." Church History 3 (1934): 267-84.

233 Newton, Joseph Fort. "Thomas Jefferson and the Religion of American Life." Forum 78 (1927): 890-896.

234 Paschall, G. Spurgeon. "Jefferson and the Baptists." Quarterly Review 15 (1955): 54-56.

235 Pearson, Samuel C. "Nature's God: A Reassessment of the Religion of the Founding Fathers." Religion in Life 46 (1977): 152-165.

236 Plochl, Willibald M. "Thomas Jefferson, Author of the Statute of Virginia for Religious Freedom." The Jurist 3 (April 1943): 182-230.

237 Powell, E.P. "Thomas Jefferson and Religion." The Open Court 10 (1896): 4943-4945.

238 Rager, John C. "Catholic Sources and the Declaration of Independence." Catholic Mind 28 (July 8, 1930): 253-268.

239 Remsburg, John Eleazer. "Thomas Jefferson" in Six Historic Americans. New York: Truth Seeker Co., 1906. pp. 65-96.

240 Sandler, S. Gerald. "Lockean Ideas in Thomas Jefferson's Bill for Establishing Religious Freedom." Journal of the History of Ideas 21 (1960): 110-116.

241 Sanford, Charles B. The Religious Life of Thomas Jefferson. Charlottesville: University Press of Virginia, 1985.

242 Schaff, David S. "The Bellarmine-Jefferson Legend and the Declaration of Independence." Papers of the American Society of Church History 2nd ser. 8 (1928): 239-276.

243 Schulz, Constance B. "The Radical Religious Ideas of Thomas Jefferson and John Adams: A Comparison." Ph.D. dissertation. University of Cincinnati, 1973.

244 Stowe, Walter H. "The Religion of Thomas Jefferson." Historical Magazine of the Protestant Episcopal Church 21 (1952): 413-415.

245 Swancara, Frank. Thomas Jefferson vs. Religious Oppression. New York: University Books, 1969.

246 Trainor, M. Rosaleen. "Thomas Jefferson on Freedom of Conscience." Ph.D. dissertation. St. John's University, 1966.

247 Wettstein, A. Arnold. "Regionless Religion in the Letters and Papers from Monticello." Religion in Life 45 (1976): 152-160.

248 Wicks, Elliott K. "Thomas Jefferson—A Religious Man With a Passion for Religious Freedom." Historical Magazine of the Protestant Episcopal Church 36 (1967): 271-283.

249 Zwierlein, Frederick J. "Thomas Jefferson and Freedom of Religion." American Ecclesiastical Review 109 (1943): 39-58.

ANDREW JOHNSON

About Andrew Johnson's religion little is known and less has been written. He never united with a church but attended Methodist services often. He believed in God and respected the Bible.

As Chief Executive during the charged atmosphere of Reconstruction, his conciliatory policies toward the South made him an object of hatred among Northern Protestant clergy, who rarely missed an opportunity to castigate him. It was this experience that drove him to attend Roman Catholic services at old St. Patrick's Church in Washington because, at least, there he would not hear political sermons!

Johnson had always been sympathetic to the Catholic Church. As a freshman Congressman from Tennessee, he defended Catholics from Know-Nothing and Nativist charges that all Catholics were traitors. His address was an eloquent one. Later in life, he sent his son to Georgetown University, Washington's famed Jesuit college.

His 1868 Christmas proclamation granting pardon and amnesty to all who had fought for the Confederacy was an act of Christian compassion and courage all too rare in an era of hatred.

See Bonnell, item 3, pp. 116-119.

See Fuller, item 8, pp. 117-124.

See Hampton, V., item 10, pp. 234-241.

See Hampton, W., item 11, pp. 58-60.

See Isely, item 12, pp. 131-136.

250 Brownlow, John R. "The Northern Protestant Pulpit and Andrew Johnson." Southern Speech and Communications Journal 39 (1974): 248-259.

LYNDON JOHNSON

Lyndon Johnson came from a Disciples of Christ tradition but he attended churches of many denominations and never really allied himself with any. His wife and children were Episcopalians, though daughter Luci became a Roman Catholic in 1965.

Johnson seemed to have had a utilitarian approach to religion. Whatever worked was fine with him, and he respected all religions. He frequently attended Episcopal and Catholic services with family members. He was once rebuked from the pulpit of an Episcopal Church in Williamsburg, Virginia because of his Vietnam policies. On another occasion he was criticized for receiving Communion in an Episcopal Church, though he was not a member.

No thorough, serious investigation of LBJ's religion has yet been published. The Fuller-Green volume contains the most information.

See Bonnell, item 3, pp. 232-236.

See Fuller, item 8, pp. 224-229.

251 Bird, John. "Lyndon Johnson's Religion." Saturday Evening Post (March 27, 1965): 81+.

252 Eller, Vernard. "Another Catholic in the White House." Christian Century 82 (August 18, 1965): 1007-1008.

253 "If Lynda Byrd Marries a Roman Catholic." Life 57 (1964): 53-54.

254 "Johnson's Faith." Time 83 (1964): 65.

255 Landsdowne, Stuart. "Where President Johnson Goes to Church." America 111 (1969): 443.

256 "LBJ Turning Catholic?" *Christianity Today* 12 (1968): 38.

257 Robertson, Nan. "Why the President's Daughter Turned to the Catholic Church." *Ladies Home Journal* 82 (August 1965): 76.

JOHN F. KENNEDY

Our nation's only Catholic President looms large in history because of the way in which he defused historic Catholic-Protestant animosities and mitigated some long-standing church-state disputes. His narrow victory, coming as it did over fierce and strident opposition, was a milestone in U.S. political and religious history.

Lawrence Fuchs, a professor at Brandeis University, produced a first-rate study of Kennedy's relationship to his church and his country. Menendez looks at Kennedy's personal religion and concludes that he was a loyal Catholic but one who emphasized the progressive, conciliatory and humanistic strains within Catholic thought. Menendez also concentrates on the church-state issues during the Kennedy Presidency and includes an appendix of JFK's major religious addresses. Schneider concentrates on Kennedy's public statements regarding religion and morality while Settel includes many of JFK's favorite biblical passages.

The volumes by Barrett and Michener are the best to consult for the drama and excitement of the religious aspects of the 1960 campaign. Flamini looks at Kennedy and the Vatican. Recent research by James Wolfe is also challenging and somewhat revisionist in posture.

For other material on the 1960 campaign see Albert J. Menendez, Religious Conflict in America: A Bibliography (New York: Garland Publishing Inc., 1985): 61-63.

See Bonnell, item 3, pp. 226-230.

See Fuller, item 8, pp. 219-223.

258   Barrett, Patricia. "Religion and the 1960 Presidential Election." Social Order 12 (June 1962): 267-285.

259   Briggs, Linda L. "The Religious Issue in the 1960 Presidential Campaign in Texas." M.A. thesis. Lamar State College, 1969.

260 "The Church and the President." *America* 106 (January 13, 1962): 2-6.

261 "Church-State Legacy of JFK." *Journal of Church and State* 6 (Winter 1964): 5-11.

262 Converse, Phillip E. *Religion and Politics: The 1960 Election.* Ann Arbor: University of Michigan Survey Research Center, 1961.

263 Flamini, Roland. *Pope, Premier and President.* New York: Macmillan, 1980.

264 Fuchs, Lawrence H. *John F. Kennedy and American Catholicism.* New York: Meredith Press, 1967.

265 Hardon, John A. "A Catholic in the White House." *Homiletic and Pastoral Review* 60 (September 1960): 1134-1140.

266 Hoyt, Robert. "Kennedy, Catholicism and the Presidency." *Jubilee* 20 (December 1960): 13-15.

267 James E.S. "Forty Minutes with President Kennedy." *Baptist Standard* (November 27, 1963): 1.

268 Kemper, Deane Alwyn. "John F. Kennedy Before the Greater Houston Ministerial Association, September 12, 1960: The Religious Issue." Ph.D. dissertation. Michigan State University, 1968.

269 Kim, Richard C. "A Roman Catholic President in the American Schema." *Journal of Church and State* 3 (May 1961): 33-40.

270 Macropoulos, Elias. "The Treatment, with Reference to the Roman Catholic Issue, of the Democratic Candidates in the Presidential Elections of 1928 and 1960, by Selected American Periodicals." Ed.D. dissertation. New York University, 1967.

271 Menendez, Albert J. *John F. Kennedy: Catholic and Humanist.* Buffalo: Prometheus Books, 1979.

272 ------. "Was Kennedy Sincere About Church-State Separation?" *Church & State* 30 (November 1977): 12-15.

273 Michener, James A. *Report of the County Chairman.* New York: Random House, 1961.

274 Pike, James A. *A Roman Catholic in the White House.* New York: Doubleday, 1960.

275 Rowland, Kathleen. "Mr. Kennedy Didn't Want Any Fuss" in *The Universe Book 1965*, edited by Piers Compton. London: Hale, 1964. pp. 170-172.

276 Schneider, Nicholas A., ed. *Religious Views of President John F. Kennedy in His Own Words.* St. Louis: Herder, 1965.

277 Settel, T.S., ed. *The Faith of JFK.* New York: Dutton, 1965.

278 Walker, David Ellis, Jr. "Invention in Selected Sermons of Ministers Opposing the Election of a Roman Catholic Presidential Candidate in 1960." M.A. thesis. University of Florida, 1961.

279 Wolfe, James Snow. "The Kennedy Myth: American Civil Religion in the 60's." Ph.D. dissertation. Graduate Theological Union, 1975.

280 ------. "The Religious Issue Revisited: Presbyterian Responses to Kennedy's Presidential Campaign." *Journal of Presbyterian History* 57 (1979): 1-18.

ABRAHAM LINCOLN

More has been written about Lincoln than any other President. And more has been written about Lincoln's religion. Perhaps this is true, at least partially, because Lincoln knew the Bible extraordinarily well, and wrote and expressed himself on religious matters. But he was never baptized and never joined a church. Still, the man Tolstoy once called a "Christ in miniature" is widely regarded as having been our most genuinely religious president. The anomaly of an unbaptized saint in the White House has long intrigued scholars and religious writers.

In Lincoln's early professional life, rumors circulated that he was a skeptic or agnostic in matters religious. His law partner, William Herndon, attested to that in his volume of reminiscences years after Lincoln's death. But if that was true, did Lincoln's views change or evolve? That is the heart of the Lincoln religious controversy. Albert House's article is a good place to start.

Even after 65 years, William Barton's The Soul of Abraham Lincoln is probably the best overall study of Lincoln's religious character. William Wolf's The Almost Chosen People is another excellent study, cautious in its conclusions. The volume by John Wesley Hill is thorough and interesting, though too hagiographic.

Quaker scholar Elton Trueblood's penetrating analysis, seeing Lincoln as "Theologian of American Anguish," is helpful, though not all of his conclusions are widely accepted by Lincoln scholars. Edgar DeWitt Jones's Lincoln and the Preachers is delightful, concentrating as it does on Lincoln's varied relationships with clergy from many traditions. His volume is replete with unusual information, e.g., that five U.S. churches have stained-glass windows commemorating the martyred President.

Joseph Lewis and John Remsburg try to prove that Lincoln was an agnostic foe of religion, while G. Frederick

Owens and William Johnstone try just as hard to claim Lincoln as a "born-again" evangelical. Neither view seems convincing.

Lincoln's "Catholic" connection has been probed by several authors, including Blied, Fish, Hurley, Meehan, Tansey and Tegeder. Lincoln grew up in a heavily Catholic part of Kentucky and several aunts and cousins were devout Catholics, including an aunt who was a mother superior of a convent. Thus, rumors arose concerning Lincoln's possible Catholicism, which all historians have rejected. (Several other churches have also claimed Lincoln, to no avail.)

But anti-Catholic extremists, beginning with the bitter ex-priest Charles Chiniquy and Brigadier General Thomas Harris, who served on the military tribunal trying the conspirators in Lincoln's assassination, claimed that Catholics masterminded the plot to kill the President. This absurd view, rejected by all historians, was advanced by Harris, McCarty and McLoughlin (who wrote his diatribe just before John Kennedy's death). See Hanchett's volume on Lincoln conspiracy theories. Greenbie's volume on Anna Ella Carroll is also worth consulting. Carroll was author of a famous anti-Catholic book published during the 1856 Presidential campaign. This charming but emotional Marylander, a Know-Nothing campaign manager, later became President Lincoln's unofficial adviser on Civil War military strategy.

For Lincoln's role as an exponent of civil religion, see Endy, Erickson, Lippy, Mead and Wiest. For his relationships with his parents' Baptist community, see Crisman and Oliver. Lincoln's use of the Bible in personal devotions and in political oratory is explored by Jackson and Macartney. Good overviews of his religious character were penned by neo-orthodox theologian, Reinhold Niebuhr, and evangelical historian, Mark Noll.

For a descent into silliness, see Grierson, Maynard, and Robbins, who all tried to prove that Lincoln was a spiritualist and mystic.

See Bonnell, item 3, pp. 108-113.

See Fuller, item 8, pp. 101-116.

See Hampton, V., item 10, pp. 231-234; pp. 344-353.

See Hampton, W., item 11, pp. 51-57.

See Isely, item 12, 123-128.

281 Abbott, Lyman. "Abraham Lincoln's Religion." Outlook 113 (June 7, 1916): 330-331.

282 ------. "Agnosticism of Abraham Lincoln." Outlook 84 (November 17, 1906): 654-655.

283 Banks, Louis Albert. The Religious Life of Famous Americans. New York: American Tract Society, 1904. pp. 3-13.

284 Barton, Bruce. "Faith of Abraham Lincoln, A Lesson for Today." Vital Speeches 6 (March 1, 1940): 290-294.

285 Barton, William E. The Soul of Abraham Lincoln. New York: Doran, 1920.

286 Bates, William H. The Religious Opinions and Life of Abraham Lincoln. Washington, D.C., 1914.

287 Beardslee, C.S. Abraham Lincoln's Cardinal Traits: A Study in Ethics, With an Epilogue Addressed to Theologians. Boston: Gorham Press, 1914.

288 Blied, Benjamin J. "Catholic Reaction to the Death of Lincoln." Salesianum 34 (1939): 72-79.

289 Bullard, F. Lauriston. "The Religion of Lincoln." The Magazine of History 34 (1927): 6-10.

290 Chittenden, L.E. "The Faith of President Lincoln." Harpers 82 (February 1891): 385-391.

291 Clancy, T.H. "Lincoln's Almost Chosen People." America 124 (February 13, 1971): 145-147.

292 Clark, Bayard S. "A Sermon by Phillips Brooks on the Death of Abraham Lincoln." Historical Magazine of the Protestant Episcopal Church 49 (March 1980): 37-49.

293 Collis, Charles H.T. The Religion of Abraham Lincoln. New York: Dillingham, 1900.

294 Cronkhite, L.G. "The Church Lincoln Didn't Join." Christian Century 52 (February 6, 1935): 170-172.

295 Crismon, L.T. "The Lincoln Family and the Baptists." Review and Expositor 57 (January 1960): 69-73.

296 DeCleyre, Voltairine. "A Lance for Anarchy." Open Court 5 (1891): 2963-2965.

297 "Did Abraham Lincoln Believe in Christianity?" Current Opinion 63 (October 1917): 262-263.

298 "Early Faith." American Catholic Historical Researches 22 (195): 211-213.

299 Endy, Melvin B., Jr. "Abraham Lincoln and American Civil Religion: A Reincarnation." Church History 44 (June 1975): 229-241.

300 Erickson, Gary Lee. "Lincoln's Civil Religion and the Lutheran Heritage." Lincoln Herald 75 (Winter 1973): 158-171.

301 Fish, C.R. "Lincoln and Catholicism." American History Review 29 (July 1924): 723-724.

302 Fox, Gresham George. Abraham Lincoln's Religion. New York: Exposition Press, 1959.

303 Fuller, Edmund and David Green. "Lincoln: Crucified President." Sign 48 (February 1969): 22-25.

304 Good, Douglas. "Abraham Lincoln: Paradigm of Forgiveness." Fides et Historia 15 (Spring-Summer 1983): 28-43.

305 Greenbie, Sydney and Marjorie. Anna Ella Carroll and Abraham Lincoln. Tampa: University of Tampa Press, 1952.

306 Grierson, Francis. Abraham Lincoln, A Practical Mystic. New York: Lane, 1918.

307 Gurley, Phineas D. "The Funeral Sermon of Abraham Lincoln." Journal of the Presbyterian Historical Society 39 (June 1961): 65-75.

308 Hanchette, William. The Lincoln Murder Conspiracies. Urbana: University of Illinois, 1984. pp. 233-244.

309 Harris, Thomas M. Rome's Responsibility for the Assassination of Abraham Lincoln. Los Angeles: Heritage Manor, 1960 [1897].

310 Hill, John Wesley. Abraham Lincoln: Man of God. New York: Putnams, 1920.

311 Horner, Harlan Hoyt. The Growth of Lincoln's Faith. New York: Abingdon, 1939.

312 House, Albert V. "The Genesis of the Lincoln Religious Controversy." Proceedings of the Middle States Association of History and Social Science Teachers 36 (1939): 44-54.

313 Howard, F. "Was Abraham Lincoln an Agnostic?" Action 7 (February 1954): 27-28.

314 Hurley, Doran. "Lincoln's Catholic Kinship." Columbia 37 (February 1957): 21-22.

315 Irwin, B.F. "Lincoln's Religious Beliefs." Illinois State Journal (May 16, 1874).

316 Jackson, John R. "An Historical and Theological Assessment of the Religious Views of Abraham Lincoln." Ph.D. dissertation. Calvin Theological Seminary, 1983.

317 Jackson, S. Trevena. Lincoln's Use of the Bible. New York: Eaton & Maine, 1909.

318 Johnstone, William J. Abraham Lincoln, the Christian. New York: Abingdon, 1913.

319 ------. How Lincoln Prayed. New York: Abingdon, 1913.

320 Jones, Edgar DeWitt. Lincoln and the Preachers. New York: Harper, 1948.

321 Kirby, J.E. "The Bishop Who Almost Stood With Lincoln." Methodist History 7 (October 1968): 31-33.

322 Lane, T.A. "Lincoln Leaned on God." Ave Maria 70 (July 2, 1949): 24.

323 Lewis, Joseph. Lincoln, The Freethinker. New York: Lincoln Publishing Co., 1924.

324 "Lincoln's Reliance on God." Catholic Educational Review 32 (February 1934): 112-113.

325 Lindstrom, Ralph G. Lincoln Finds God. New York: Longmans, 1958.

326 Lippy, Charles H. "The President as Priest: Civil Religion and the American Presidency." Journal of Religious Studies 8 (Fall 1980): 29-41.

327 Logan, Thomas D. "Lincoln's Religious Faith and Principles." The Interior (February 11, 1909).

328 Ludwig, Charles. "Lincoln and His Pastor." Christianity Today 10 (January 21, 1966): 15-16.

329 Lynch, John. "Lincoln's Religion." Priest 16 (February 1960): 158-163.

330 Macartney, Clarence. Lincoln and the Bible. New York: Abingdon, 1949.

331 Malone, T.J. "Where Lincoln Got Under God." Columbia 32 (September 1952): 7+.

332 Maynard, Nettie Colburn. Was Abraham Lincoln a Spiritualist? Philadelphia: Rufus Hartranft, 1891.

333 McCarty, Burke. The Suppressed Truth About the Assassination of Abraham Lincoln. Haverhill, Ma.: Arya Varta, 1964 [1924].

334 McCollister, J. "The Faith of Abe Lincoln." Saturday Evening Post 255 (January/February 1983): 46-47.

335 McCrie, George M. "What Was Abraham Lincoln's Creed?" Open Court 5 (1891): 3031-3033.

336 McLoughlin, Emmett. An Inquiry Into the Assassination of Abraham Lincoln. New York: Lyle Stuart, 1963.

337 McMurtrie, Douglas C. Lincoln's Religion. Chicago: Black Cat Press, 1936.

338 Mead, Sidney E. "Abraham Lincoln's Last Best Hope of Earth: The American Dream of Destiny and Democracy" Church History 23 (March 1954): 3-16.

339 Meehan, Thomas F. "Lincoln's Opinion of Catholics." United States Catholic Historical Society Records and Studies 16 (1924): 87-93.

340 Morgenthau, Hans J. and David Hein. Essays on Lincoln's Faith and Politics. Lanham, Md.: University Press of America, 1983.

341 "New Lights on Abraham Lincoln's Religion." Current Opinion 68 (April 1920): 515-518.

342 Nicolay, John G. and John Hay. "Lincoln and the Church." Century 38 (August 1889): 559-568.

343 Niebuhr, Reinhold. "The Religion of Abraham Lincoln." Christian Century 82 (February 10, 1965): 172-175.

344 Noll, Mark A. "The Perplexing Faith of Abraham Lincoln." Christianity Today 29 (February 15, 1985): 12-16.

345 Oliver, Henry. "Cap'n Abraham Linkhorn's Church: Long Run Baptist Church, Jefferson County, Ky." American Mercury 77 (August 1953): 69.

346 Owen, George Frederick. Abraham Lincoln: The Man and His Faith. Wheaton: Tyndale House, 1981. Originally published as A Heart That Yearned For God. Washington, D.C.: Third Century Publications, 1976.

347 Pennell, Orrin Henry. Religious Views of Abraham Lincoln. Alliance, Oh.: R.M. Scanton, 1899.

348 Peters, Madison C. Abraham Lincoln's Religion. Boston: Gorham, 1909.

349 Randall, J.G. "Lincoln's Greatest Declaration of Faith." The New York Times Magazine (February 6, 1949): 11.

350 Randall, R.P. "Lincoln's Faith Was Born of Anguish." The New York Times Magazine (February 7, 1954): 11.

351 Reed, James A. "The Later Life and Religious Sentiments of Abraham Lincoln." Scribners Monthly 7 (1893): 333-334.

352 Reeves, Robert N. *Abraham Lincoln, His Religion.* Chicago: H.L. Green, 1903.

353 Remsburg, John E. *Abraham Lincoln: Was He A Christian?* New York: Truth Seeker, 1893.

354 Robbins, Peggy. "The Lincolns and Spiritualism." *Civil War Times Illustrated* 15 (August 1976): 4-10.

355 Robinson, L.E. "Lincoln's Religion Restated." *Bookman* 51 (July 1920): 547-552.

356 Roger, R.C. "The Religious Beliefs of Abraham Lincoln." *Open Court* 5 (1891): 3037-3039.

357 Settle, R.W. "Abraham Lincoln's Faith." *Christianity Today* 2 (February 3, 1958): 6-8.

358 Smith, T.V. *Lincoln and the Spiritual Life.* Boston: Beacon Press, 1951.

359 Speakman, Frederick B. "Can The Church Join Abraham Lincoln?" *Princeton Seminary Bulletin* 68 (Winter 1976): 24-27.

360 Sperry, Willard L. *The Meaning of God in the Life of Lincoln.* Boston: Central Church, 1922.

361 Starr, John William. "What was Abraham Lincoln's Religion?" *Magazine of History with Notes and Queries* (1921).

362 Stern, P.V. "Lincoln's Faith." *Nation* 152 (March 8, 1941): 280.

363 Tansey, Ann. "Lincoln and the Nuns." *Information* 70 (February 1956): 2-9.

364 Tarbell, Ida. "Not a Catholic." *American Catholic Historical Researches* 22 (1905): 165-166.

365 Tegeder, V.C. "Catholic Lincolniana." *American Benedictine Review* 13 (December 1962): 596-607.

366 Thayer, George A. *The Religion of Abraham Lincoln.* Cincinnati: Ebbert and Richardson, 1909.

367 Thompson, D. "Abraham Lincoln on Temperance." *Methodist Review* 81 (1899): 9-19.

368 Trueblood, Elton. Abraham Lincoln: Theologian of American Anguish. New York: Harper, 1973.

369 Tyler, B.B. "The Religious Character of Abraham Lincoln." Homiletic Review 30 (1895): 84-89.

370 Watson, Edward L. "The Conversion of Lincoln." Christian Advocate (November 11, 1909).

371 White, Kermit E. "Abraham Lincoln and Christianity." Ph.D. dissertation. Boston University, 1954.

372 Whitelaw, David P. "A Theology of Anguish." Theological Evangelica 15 (November 1982): 38-48.

373 Wiest, Walter E. "Lincoln's Political Ethics: An Alternative to American Millenialism." American Journal of Theology and Philosophy 5 (September 1983): 116-126.

374 Wilson, Edmund. "Abraham Lincoln: The Union as Religious Mysticism." New Yorker 29 (March 14, 1953): 116.

375 Wolf, William J. The Almost Chosen People. New York: Doubleday, 1959.

376 ------. Lincoln's Religion. Philadelphia: Pilgrim, 1970.

377 ------. The Religion of Abraham Lincoln. New York: Seabury, 1963.

378 Woods, R.L. "Lincoln's Faith in God." Sign 40 (February 1961): 32-33.

379 Wright, James C. "Lincoln and the Beatitudes." Christianity Today 27 (February 4, 1983): 21.

JAMES MADISON

In his seminal volume on religion and the Founding Fathers, Norman Cousins says that Madison "referred only rarely to his personal religious beliefs." This may explain the dearth of written material concerning Madison's religion.

Madison was a liberal Episcopalian who maintained a serious, scholarly interest in theology, ethics and the Bible. He studied at Princeton and may have been influenced by the liberal Presbyterians he encountered there.

His great contribution to American history was his passionate advocacy of religious liberty, both in his native Virginia and at the Constitutional Convention. Madison, rightly called the Father of the Constitution, fought for the inclusion of religious liberty in the Federal Bill of Rights. Thus, the articles and books cited in this chapter deal with his role in separating church and state, placing a ban on the establishment of religion by government and guaranteeing the free exercise of religion to all citizens of this Republic.

As President, Madison practiced what he preached, vetoing acts incorporating the Episcopal Church in the District of Columbia and granting federal land to a Baptist church in Mississippi. He also opposed a paid chaplaincy in Congress and a question on religion in the federal census, but he reluctantly proclaimed a national day of prayer.

The Alley anthology includes essays by noted scholars on Madison's contributions. Brant, Drakeman and Hunt are also worth reading.

See Bonnell, item 3, pp. 38-41.

See Fuller, item 8, pp. 39-46.

See Hampton, V., item 10, pp. 203-207.

See Hampton, W., item 11, pp. 24-25.

See Isely, item 12, pp. 27-32.

380 Alley, Robert, ed. James Madison on Religious Liberty. Buffalo: Prometheus Books, 1985.

381 Brant, Irving. "Madison on the Separation of Church and State." William and Mary Quarterly, third series, 8 (January 1951): 3-24.

382 Cousins, Norman, ed. In God We Trust. New York: Harper, 1958. pp. 295-325.

383 Drakeman, Donald L. "Religion and the Republic: James Madison and the First Amendment." Journal of Church and State 25 (Autumn 1983): 427-445.

384 Drouin, Edmond G. "Madison and Jefferson on Clergy in the Legislature." America 138 (January 28, 1978): 58-59.

385 Hunt, Gaillard. James Madison and Religious Liberty. Washington, D.C.: Government Printing Office, 1902.

WILLIAM MCKINLEY

William McKinley was a devout evangelical Methodist who conceived of political activity as one way of serving Christian aims. McKinley was particularly interested in missionary endeavors and world evangelization, though he once clumsily justified the U.S. takeover of the Philippines by claiming that we were going to "Christianize" the natives who had been Christian for over 300 years. (McKinley once called Christianity "the mightiest factor in the world's civilization.")

Unlike many evangelicals, he was not notably anti-Catholic. His relations with Catholics were cordial, and he appointed several to top positions. His foreign policy toward Catholic countries, though, made him unpopular in some Catholic circles, and his Catholic vote, the highest ever for a Republican in 1896, declined somewhat in 1900. (See Frank T. Reuter's book cited below.)

His personal devoutness, his tenderness toward his epileptic wife, his public forgiveness of his assassin and the dignity of his death made McKinley's popularity soar among church-going Americans.

See Bonnell, item 3, pp. 158-163.

See Fuller, item 8, pp. 157-161.

See Hampton, V., item 10, pp. 250-257; pp. 356-359.

See Hampton, W., item 11, pp. 76-78.

See Isely, item 12, pp. 187-192.

386 Banks, Louis Albert. <u>The Religious Life of Famous Americans</u>. New York: American Tract Society, 1904. pp. 65-74.

387 Barton, Frederick. "A Christian Gentleman, William McKinley." <u>The Chautauquan</u> 34 (November 1901): 134-138.

388 McKinley, William. "Welcome from the Nation to the Ecumenical Conference." *Missionary Review of the World* 23 (1900): 410.

389 Reuter, Frank T. *Catholic Influence on American Colonial Policies 1898-1904.* Austin: University of Texas Press, 1967.

JAMES MONROE

Monroe was the fourth Virginia Episcopalian (if we count Jefferson) to serve as president during the infancy of our Republic. An able man who was fortunate enough to preside over an "era of good feeling," Monroe kept his religion to himself. Therefore, no one has written much about it.

He faithfully attended St. John's Church near the White House. His marriage and funeral were conducted under Episcopal auspices. The Episcopal Bishop of New York conducted his funeral service.

Monroe seemed to be uncomfortable with public religious utterances, and rarely made any.

See Bonnell, item 3, pp. 44-47.

See Fuller, item 8, pp. 47-51.

See Hampton, V., item 10, pp. 207-213.

See Hampton, W., item 11, p. 26.

See Isely, item 12, pp. 35-40.

RICHARD NIXON

Nixon was a "California" Quaker whose religious upbringing was standard evangelical rather than traditional Eastern Quaker. Nixon told readers of Billy Graham's Decision magazine that he had "committed his life to Christ and Christian service" at an evangelical tent rally in California in the 1920's. Later, he taught Sunday School to high school students.

As president, Nixon inaugurated the custom of holding regular services at the White House. Nixon hoped it would become a "White House institution."

In his introduction to a collection of sermons delivered during the first two years of these formal events, Nixon told why he did it.

"When I was elected to the highest office in the land, I decided that I wanted to do something to encourage attendance at services and to emphasize this country's basic faith in a Supreme Being. It seemed to me that one way of achieving this was to set a good example. What better example could there be than to bring the worship service, with all its solemn meaning, right into the White House?"

"Symbolically, I have regarded our White House services as a standing invitation to all men and women of good will to participate--in their own place and their own way--in the 'answer of the spirit' which this nation so urgently needs."

Nixon's pal Billy Graham was the lead-off preacher in 1969. The services were held 26 times during the first two years, about once a month. Then they tapered off.

Nixon selected the clergy and while he did balance them among Protestant denominations, Catholics and Jews, he tended to select "safe" conservatives who would not utter a word of criticism of his increasingly controversial policies. The sermons were largely pietistic, personal and nonpolitical, except when Norman Vincent Peale defended Nixon's policies in Vietnam.

Critics excoriated Nixon for mixing church and state, for creating a captive audience and for trying to cloak partisanship in civil religion. (See Novak and Fiske.)

Nixon's involvement in the Watergate scandal was the occasion for much soul-searching among theologians, especially liberal ones. (See Moellering.) Nixon critics regarded his religious affirmations as exercises in hypocrisy.

Nixon's fellow Quakers were incensed by his Vietnam policies and many tried to expel him from fellowship. (See Coffin and Mayer.) Nixon was a very nondenominational Quaker. As Vice President, he attended a Methodist church in Washington. As a New York businessman, he frequented Norman Vincent Peale's Marble Collegiate Church, a parish of the Reformed Church of America.

As president, Nixon attended a Billy Graham rally in Tennessee and received the "Churchman of the Year" award from Religious Heritage of America--which incensed his many critics.

The Henderson book is the most thorough and complete look at Nixon's religion. Donahue, Strachan, Mills and Wimberly are also recommended.

See Bonnell, item 3, pp. 238-244.

390   Coffin, T.E. "Richard Nixon and the Quaker Fellowship." Christian Century 91 (January 2, 1974): 5-6.

391   Chandler, Russell. "National Prayer Breakfast: Powerful Audience." Christianity Today 15 (February 26, 1971): 40+.

392   "Christmas at the Nixon's." Time 94 (December 26, 1969): 6-7.

393   "Churchman of the Year." Newsweek 75 (May 25, 1970): 96.

394   Donahue, Bernard F. "The Political Use of Religious Symbols: A Case Study of the 1972 Presidential Campaign." Review of Politics 37 (1975): 48-65.

395 Doyle, Barrie. "The Religious Campaign." Christianity Today 17 (October 27, 1972): 34-38.

396 Fiske, Edward. "Praying with the President in the White House." New York Times Magazine (August 8, 1971): 14-15.

397 "God and the White House." Newsweek 74 (July 14, 1969): 57.

398 Henderson, Charles P., Jr. The Nixon Theology. New York: Harper and Row, 1972.

399 ------. "Richard Nixon, Theologian." Nation 211 (September 21, 1970): 232-236.

400 Huffman, Kenneth. "Sunday at the White House: Watchers and Worshipers." Christianity Today 13 (August 22, 1969): 38-39.

401 "In Praise of Youth: Nixon's Appearance at Billy Graham's East Tennessee Crusade." Time 95 (June 8, 1970): 13.

402 Kramer, Michael. "Is Nixon Kosher?" New York 5 (August 14, 1972): 26-33.

403 Mayer, Milton. "Disownment; the Quakers and Their President." Christian Century 90 (October 10, 1973): 1000-1003.

404 McWilliams, Carey. "The Church-State Issue." Nation 214 (April 24, 1972): 515-516.

405 Moellering, Ralph. "Civil Religion, the Nixon Theology and the Watergate Scandal." Christian Century 90 (September 26, 1973): 947-950.

406 Nixon, Richard M. "A Nation's Faith in God." Decision 3 (November 1962): 4.

407 "Nixon and the Church." Christianity Today 18 (February 1, 1974): 43-44.

408 "Nixon and God." Nation 218 (June 15, 1974): 738.

409 Novak, Michael. "White House Religion: A Tricky Business." Christian Century 87 (September 23, 1970): 1112.

410 Osborne, John. "Blessed Assurance; Attendance at Billy Graham's Crusade in Knoxville, Tennessee." The New Republic 162 (June 13, 1970): 11-13.

411 "Preaching and the Power; Billy Graham and the White House." Newsweek 76 (July 20, 1970): 50-55.

412 "Rabbi's Prayer About Nixon." U.S. News and World Report 67 (July 14, 1969): 12.

413 "Religious Services with the Nixons." U.S. News and World Report 66 (February 10, 1969): 11.

414 Strachan, Jill Penelope. "Richard Nixon: Representative Religious American." Ph.D. dissertation. Syracuse University, 1981.

415 Swomley, John M. "Manipulating the Blocs: Church, State and Mr. Nixon." Nation 215 (September 11, 1972): 168-171.

416 Wills, Garry. "How Nixon Used the Media, Billy Graham, and the Good Lord to Rap with Students at Tennessee University." Esquire 74 (September 1970): 119-122.

417 Wimberly, Ronald C. "Civil Religion and the Choice for President: Nixon in '72." Social Forces 59 (1980): 44-61.

418 Woodward, Kenneth L. "White House Sermons." Newsweek 79 (May 22, 1972): 60.

419 "Worship in the East Room." Time 94 (June 11, 1969): 48.

FRANKLIN PIERCE

Franklin Pierce was a lonely, dejected president whose policies were unpopular and whose wife was something of a religious fanatic. Sorrow followed them everywhere. Two sons died in childhood. Their pride and joy, Benjamin, the third son, was killed in a train wreck before their very eyes a few weeks before Inauguration Day. This cast a pall over the Pierce White House. Mrs. Pierce, obsessed with the idea that God was punishing her, wore black for four years and prohibited all social functions.

Both the President and First Lady sank deeper into melancholia and guilt, and Pierce drifted toward alcoholism. To compensate, both attended church (Presbyterian or Congregational) regularly, engaged in family prayers and refused to even open a letter on Sunday.

Pierce became estranged from Congregationalism because of the clergy's fanaticism on the slavery question. As a moderate Democrat, Pierce tried to conciliate the South and was therefore hated by Northern extremists. As a private citizen during the Civil War, he was ostracized by his fellow New Hampshire citizens and on at least one occasion his life was threatened.

After his wife's death, he gravitated toward the Episcopal Church, which was then, like the Catholic Church, non-political. Here he could hear religious sermons, not political ones. He was baptized in 1865 and confirmed in 1866, three years before his lonely death.

Not much has been written about Pierce's religion, but Isely and Fuller are good sources.

See Bonnell, item 3, pp. 96-99.

See Fuller, item 8, pp. 92-95.

See Hampton, V., item 10, pp. 393-394.

See Hampton, W., item 11, pp. 45-46.

See Isely, item 12, pp. 107-112.

JAMES K. POLK

James Polk, one of our most underrated presidents, respected his Presbyterian traditions but gave limited thought to religion throughout most of his busy public life.

As president, Polk appointed the first Catholic chaplains for the U.S. Armed Forces--largely to deflect criticism that the Mexican War had sectarian connotations-- and was roundly criticized by some Protestant clergy for doing so. The tolerant Polk was disgusted by the religious animosities that began to sweep the country during his Presidency. He opposed a proposal to stop the Mormons from crossing the country to Utah. He refused to consider religion when making appointments. When a Presbyterian preacher denounced his appointment of Catholic chaplains for Catholic soldiers, he wrote, "Thank God, under our Constitution, there is no connection between church and state, and in my action as President of the United States, I recognized no distinction of creeds in my appointments to office."

His wife was a devoted Presbyterian who prohibited dancing and liquor in the White House. She and the President refused to do any business on Sunday unless it were crucial. He and his wife attended church regularly.

But Polk preferred the Methodist Church, probably as a result of a sermon he heard at a camp meeting in 1833. On his deathbed in 1849 he sent for the preacher, John McFerrin, and asked for baptism. He had been a true workaholic as president, never taking a real vacation, and died of the effects of strain and overwork just three months after leaving office.

The Polk chapter in Earl West's doctoral dissertation is the best source for Polk's religious character.

See Bonnell, item 3, pp. 80-83.

See Fuller, item 8, pp. 81-86.

See Hampton, V., item 10, pp. 354-355.

See Hampton, W., item 11, pp. 37-42.

See Isely, item 12, pp. 83-88.

420 West, Earl Irvin. "James K. Polk: Silent Puritan." in "Religion and Politics in the Jacksonian Era." Ph.D. dissertation. Indiana University, 1968. pp. 133-157.

RONALD REAGAN

Volumes could be written--and probably will be--about Ronald Reagan's religious agenda for the 1980's and his alliance with politically active evangelicals and fundamentalists. Reagan is the first 20th-Century president to have a specific religious agenda--a ban on abortion, aid to church-related schools, a return to government-mandated school prayer. This agenda, and the accompanying polarization of religious groups favoring and opposing these initiatives, has led to the most intense conflict along religious lines in decades.

Reagan is the third president to hold nominal membership in the Christian Church (Disciples of Christ), though he attends Presbyterian services on the rare occasions when he attends a church. His personal religious views seem to have evolved from a laid-back nonreflective California churchgoing style to a conservative evangelicalism, almost bordering on fundamentalism. He has expressed his absolute confidence in the integrity and literal truth of the Bible, reaffirmed traditional sexual mores, and even raised doubts about the validity of scientific evolution. He has said the Bible offers certain answers to every human predicament, and has come close to acceptance of certain fundamentalist presuppositions concerning Armageddon and the end-of-time prophecies. He has allied himself with a kind of nineteenth-century American Messianism, endorsing the "Covenant" view of the United States as a nation with a special relationship to God.

He has rarely missed an opportunity to address evangelical audiences and has specifically endorsed many of their objectives. Yet, his public persona is that of a tolerant, personable man. His relationships with the Roman Catholic community and with many Cardinals is cordial. His Administration is heavily Catholic in staff, more so than any previous Republican one. He restored U.S. diplomatic relations with the Holy See. His supporters say he is restoring religion to an honored place in American public life and law. His critics see his Administration as the worst in history in religious matters, saying he has a fundamental misunderstanding of the role religion is supposed to play in the public life of the first nation in history to constitutionally separate the institutions of church and state. Some critics believe he has unleashed a new era of bigotry and religious conflict that will endure for decades to come.

Richard Pierard and Robert Linder have done splendid research on Reagan's religious roots, his political cultivation of the evangelical community, and his use of civil religion to buttress right-wing goals. Other critical looks at the Reagan-evangelical entente can be found in Buie, Conn, Menendez, Blumenthal, Bole, Castelli, Collum and Wallis.

Evangelical admirers of Reagan include Dugan, LaHaye, and Wead. An excellent academic study was done by Fairbanks.

Some excellent overviews of the religious factors in the 1984 election include John Herbers' fine articles in the New York Times and Sidney Blumenthal's New Republic article. The Menendez article "Religion at the Polls, 1984" looks at the religious vote in 1984 and weighs the evidence for and against realignment. Also see James Reichley, a political scientist who agrees that America is heading for a confessional party system.

Two of the most unbelievable campaign books ever published in U.S. history must be cited because they typify the bias of the evangelical community toward Mr. Reagan. Tyndale House, an evangelical publisher in Wheaton, Illinois, published David Shepherd's Ronald Reagan: In God I Trust, a collection of Reagan's public comments on religion and morality. Shepherd stopped just short of declaring Reagan God's anointed candidate. He hailed Reagan's policies as biblical and claimed that God would bless America as long as Reagan was president. Nowhere on the book's cover did the publisher inform readers that Shepherd was a Republican campaign worker in Nashville.

Bob Slosser, a former New York Times reporter and born-again zealot who is now Vice President of the Christian Broadcasting Network, published a pro-Reagan tract (Reagan: Inside Out) through Word Publishers. Slosser's superstitious, bigoted garbage has to be read to be believed. It may be unique in the annals of campaign literature, claiming as it does that God Almighty Himself appeared to Reagan in a Sacramento hotel room in 1970, in the company of popsinger Pat Boone and several fundamentalist preachers. The Lord is supposed to have anointed Reagan for higher office if the California governor adhered to strict policies of moral reformation for the American nation. The book, widely distributed in evangelical circles, clearly portrayed the 1984 election as a choice between God and Satan.

For additional titles concerning the 1980 campaign, see Albert J. Menendez, *Religious Conflict in America: A Bibliography* (New York: Garland Publishing, Inc. 1985): 111-117.

421 Blumenthal, Sidney. "The Righteous Empire." *New Republic* 191 (October 22, 1984): 18-24.

422 Bole, William. "Is the G.O.P. Becoming God's Own Party?" *Church & State* 38 (January 1985): 12-13.

423 Buie, Jim. "Praise the Lord and Pass the Ammunition." *Church & State* 37 (October 1984): 4-8.

424 Buie, Jim and Joseph Conn. "The Bishops and the Ballot Box." *Church & State* 37 (November 1984): 4-7.

425 ------. "Campaign 84: The Crusade for America's Soul." *Church & State* 37 (September 1984): 4-8.

426 Carey, Joseph. "Religion and Politics: Furor Keeps Building." *U.S. News & World Report* 97 (September 17, 1984): 29-30.

427 Castelli, Jim. "Religious Abuses in the Reagan Administration." *Christian Century* 102 (May 22, 1985): 526-528.

428 Clapp, Rodney. "The God and Politics Debate—How the Press Got Religion." *Christianity Today* 28 (December 14, 1984): 26-29.

429 Clendinen, Dudley. "TV Evangelists Assume Larger Convention Role." *New York Times* (August 19, 1984).

430 Clymer, Adam. "Religion and Politics Mix Poorly for Democrats." *New York Times* (November 25, 1984).

431 Coleman, Milton. "Mondale Warns Against Mixing Politics, Religion." *Washington Post* (August 28, 1984): A4.

432 Collum, Danny. "An Ill Wind in Dallas." *Sojourners* 13 (October 1984): 5.

433 ------. "Reagan's Election Crusade." *Sojourners* 13 (April 1984): 4-5.

434 ------. "What's At Stake...And What Isn't." *Sojourners* 13 (September 1984): 12-21.

435 Conn, Joseph. "President Reagan's Old Time Gospel Hour." *Church & State* 38 (March 1985): 4-8.

436 ------. "Reagan Backs Government Sponsored School Prayer." *Church & State* 35 (June 1982): 3, 21-22.

437 ------. "There He Goes Again: Reagan Launches Election-Year Crusade on Church-State Issues." *Church & State* 37 (March 1984): 10-12.

438 ------. "The Vatican Connection." *Church & State* 37 (February 1984): 4-7.

439 Cuomo, Mario. "Of Faith and Freedom." *Church & State* 37 (November 1984): 8-11.

440 Dawidowicz, Lucy. "Politics, the Jews and the '84 Election." *Commentary* (February 1985): 25-30.

441 DeWitt, John. "Jewish Leader Criticizes Reagan on Church-State Campaign Issue." *Arizona Daily Star* (September 18, 1984).

442 Dickenson, James R. "Abortion Issue Draws Church Leaders Into Presidential Push." *Washington Post* (September 16, 1984): A7.

443 ------. "Cuomo Challenges Catholics." *Washington Post* (September 14, 1984): A1, A6.

444 ------. "Religion is Powerful GOP Theme." *Washington Post* (August 24, 1984).

445 DiVeroli, Robert. "Jewish Community Feels Threatened by Evangelical Movement." *San Diego Tribune* (March 16, 1985).

446 ------. "Religious Groups Offer Election Score Cards." *San Diego Tribune* (November 3, 1984): A14-A15.

447 Droel, William M. and Pierce, Gregory F. "The Catholic Vote." *Commonweal* 120 (September 7, 1984): 455-456.

448 D'Souza, Dinesh. "Will the Christian Right Help Reagan?" Washington Post (August 19, 1984): B1, B4.

449 Dugan, Robert P., Jr. "Election '84: Some Surprising Winners and Losers." Christianity Today 28 (January 18, 1985): 40-44.

450 Dunnam, Spurgeon M., III. "The Great 1984 'Religion and Politics' Debate: Some Conclusions." United Methodist Reporter (October 5, 1984): 2.

451 Elbert, David. "Poll Shows Iowans Favor No Mix of Religion, Politics." Des Moines Register (September 30, 1984): 1A, 12A.

452 Fairbanks, James David. "Reagan, Religion and the New Right." Midwest Quarterly 23 (1982): 327-345.

453 Fisher, Paul A. "Religious Values Propel Reagan Sweep." Wanderer 121 (November 15, 1984): 1, 8.

454 Frawley, Joan. "Are These Our Kind of Guys?" National Catholic Register 60 (March 18, 1984): 1.

455 ------. "For Reagan, Catholic Vote Still Elusive." National Catholic Register 60 (July 22, 1984): 1, 7.

456 Goldman, Ari L. "Rabbis Ponder the Mix of Politics and Religion." New York Times (September 13, 1984): B1, B9.

457 Gordon, Max. "Reagan, Jackson and the Jews." Jewish Currents 38 (October 1984): 4-9, 33.

458 Hays, Charlotte. "Reagan and the Catholic Vote." National Catholic Register 40 (August 19, 1984): 1, 10.

459 Herbers, John. "Armageddon View Prompts a Debate." New York Times (October 24, 1984): A1, A25.

460 ------. "Catholic Activism: Reasons and Risks." New York Times (September 23, 1984).

461 ------. "Church-State Issue May Hurt Reagan's Effort to Attract Jews." New York Times (October 18, 1984): D26.

462 ------. "Moral Majority and Its Allies Expect Harvest of Votes for Conservatives." New York Times (November 4, 1984): 38.

463 ------. "Political and Religious Shifts Rekindle Church-State Issue." New York Times (September 2, 1984): 1, 20.

464 ------. "Reagan Beginning to Get Top Billing In Christian Bookstores for Policies." New York Times (September 28, 1984): A23.

465 ------. "Religious Leaders Tell of Worry on Armageddon View Ascribed to Reagan." New York Times (October 21, 1984).

466 Hutchinson, Bob. "Prolife Democrats—Can They Influence the Leadership of the Democratic Party?" Catholic Twin Circle 21 (January 27, 1985): 3-4.

467 Hyer, Marjorie. "Campaign Rhetoric Sparks Debate Among Religious Leaders." Washington Post (September 5, 1984): A4.

468 ------. "Jewish Leader Attacks Reagan-Falwell Link." Washington Post (October 31, 1984).

469 Ingwerson, Marshall. "Fundamentalist Coalition Rallies Conservative Vote." Christian Science Monitor (November 6, 1984): 1.

470 Jaroslovsky, Rich. "Religious Right Counts on Reagan." Wall Street Journal (September 18, 1984): 64.

471 "Jewish Leaders Concerned About State-Religion Mix." St. Petersburg Independent (September 29, 1984): A6.

472 Johnson, Haynes. "Reagan Boosts Effort to Erase Line Between Church, State." Washington Post (August 26, 1985): A2.

473 Joyce, Fay S. "Mondale Explains Role for Religion." New York Times (September 8, 1984): 8.

474 Kristol, Irving. "The Political Dilemma of American Jews." Commentary (July 1984): 23-29.

475 Kurzweil, John. "How Mondale Will Appeal to Catholic Voters." Catholic Twin Circle 20 (September 9, 1984): 10-11, 17.

476 LaHaye, Tim. "The Election of Our Lifetime." Religious Broadcasting 43 (July/August 1984): 14-15.

477 Landau, Yehezkel. "The President and the Prophets." Sojourners 13 (June-July 1984): 24-25.

478 Linder, Robert. "Reagan at Kansas State: Civil Religion in the Service of the New Right." Reformed Journal 32 (December 1982): 13-15.

479 Linhardt, Arnold. "New York's Jewish Voter: Losing Clout?" Jewish Currents 38 (June 1984): 4-6.

480 Lipset, Seymour Martin. "Jews Are Still Liberals and Proud of It." Washington Post (December 30, 1984).

481 Lipset, Seymour Martin and Earl Raab. "The American Jews, the 1984 Elections and Beyond." Tocqueville Review 6 (1984): 401-419.

482 Maidens, Melinda. Religion, Morality and the New Right. New York: Facts on File, 1982.

483 McConagha, Alan. "Mondale Says GOP Intends to 'Control Your Private Life.'" Washington Times (September 24, 1984).

484 MacPherson, Myra. "Wooing the Jewish Vote." Washington Post (August 23, 1984): D1, D9.

485 Matt, A.J., Jr. "The Battle For The Souls Of America's Catholics." Wanderer 121 (August 16, 1984): 4.

486 Menendez, Albert J. "A Christmas Message From The President." Church & State 36 (December 1983): 11-12.

487 ------. "On Canonizing Reagan." Church & State 37 (May 1984): 19-20.

488 ------. "Religion at the Polls, 1984." Church & State 37 (December 1984): 7-12.

489 ------. "The Right Reverend Ronald Reagan." Church & State 36 (May 1983): 16-17.

490 Menendez, Albert J. and Jim Buie. "1984: How the Religious Blocs Stack Up." Church & State 37 (September 1984): 9-13.

491 Miller, Arthur H. and Martin P. Wattenberg. "Politics from the Pulpit: Religiosity and the 1980 Elections." Public Opinion Quarterly 48 (Spring 1984): 301-317.

492 Mills, James. "The Serious Implications of a 1971 Conversation with Ronald Reagan." San Diego Magazine 37 (August 1985): 140-141, 258.

493 "Mr. Reagan's Civil Religion." Commonweal 120 (September 21, 1984): 483-484.

494 Mondale, Walter. "Religion is a Private Matter." Church & State 37 (October 1984): 12-15.

495 Moody, Sid. "Religion Marries Politics." San Diego Union (October 21, 1984): C1, C8.

496 Mouat, Lucia. "Do Religious Issues Sway Voters?" Christian Science Monitor (September 5, 1984): 3, 4.

497 Nall, Stephanie and Thomas D. Brandt. "Archdiocese Rejects Ferraro As Speaker At Al Smith Dinner." Washington Times (October 16, 1984): 3A.

498 Oreskes, Michael. "Politicians and Religion: Discussion Signals Shift." New York Times (August 6, 1984): A14.

499 Perry, James W. "Church and State: Candidates' Views on Religion Remain Big Campaign Issue." Wall Street Journal (September 18, 1984): 1, 26.

500 Pierard, Richard V. "The Great Eclipse." Eternity 35 (February 1984): 15-19.

501 ------. "Reagan and the Evangelicals." Christian Century 100 (December 21, 1983): 1182-1185.

502 ------. "Ronald Reagan and the Evangelicals" in Fundamentalism Today ed. by Marla J. Selvidge. Elgin, Il.: Brethren Press, 1985. pp. 47-61.

503 Pierce, Kenneth M. "God and the Ballot Box." Time 124 (September 17, 1984): 26-27.

504 "Politics and the Pulpit." Newsweek 108 (September 17, 1984): 24-35.

505 Pressman, Steven. "Religious Right: Trying to Link Poll Power and Lobby Muscle." Congressional Quarterly 42 (September 22, 1984): 2315-2319.

506 Reagan, Ronald. "Religion And Politics Are Necessarily Related." Church & State 37 (October 1984): 9-11.

507 Redlich, Norman. "Some Cracks In The Wall." Nation 239 (September 29, 1984): 277-280.

508 Reichley, A. James. "Religion and Political Realignment." Brookings Review 3 (Fall 1984): 29-35.

509 Reston, James. "Reagan's Political Religion." New York Times (August 29, 1984).

510 Rodden, John. "The Religious Fellow Traveler." Commonweal 120 (September 7, 1984): 466-470.

511 Rogers, David. "Roman Catholics Are Deeply Torn by Debate Over Religion, Politics." Wall Street Journal (September 19, 1984): 1, 22.

512 Rose, William. "The Reagans and Their Pastor." Christian Life 30 (May 1968): 24-25, 44.

513 Saikowski, Charlotte. "Church-State, Religion Issues Loom in '84 Race." Christian Science Monitor (August 14, 1984): 1+.

514 Salmans, Sandra. "Christian Fundamentalists Press Own Campaign Within the G.O.P. Drive." New York Times (August 17, 1984).

515 Schanberg, Sydney H. "The G.O.P. Goes For The Jews." New York Times (October 13, 1984): 27.

516 Schlesinger, Arthur, Jr. "Church-State Rift Is As Old As America." Wall Street Journal (September 20, 1984).

517 Schneider, William. "The Jewish Vote in 1984: Elements in a Controversy." Public Opinion 7 (December 1984/January 1985): 18-19, 58.

518 Schwartz, Michael. "Catholicism Not a Political

Handicap or Advantage." Our Sunday Visitor 73 (September 2, 1984): 5.

519 Shepherd, David R. Ronald Reagan: In God I Trust. Wheaton, Il.: Tyndale House, 1984.

520 Simbro, William. "'Battle of Armageddon' Emerges As Issue In Presidential Election." Des Moines Register (October 28, 1984): 1.

521 Slosser, Bob. Reagan Inside Out. Waco: Word, 1984.

522 Sobran, Joseph. "The Entanglement of Religion, Politics." Washington Times (June 26, 1984): 2C.

523 ------. "Not a Catholic Issue." Washington Times (September 25, 1984): 2C.

524 ------. "Seeking to Reclaim the Religious Issue." Washington Times (September 20, 1984): 1C.

525 Spring, Beth. "Born-again Minnesotans Play Political Hardball." Christianity Today 28 (September 21, 1984): 68-70.

526 ------. "Rating Reagan." Christianity Today 27 (October 7, 1983): 44-49.

527 ------. "Republicans, Religion, and Reelection." Christianity Today 28 (October 5, 1984): 54-58.

528 Stern, Sol. "The Falwell Fallacy: The Limits of Fundamentalist Support for Israel." Reform Judaism 13 (Winter 1984-1985): 5-6.

529 Strobel, Warren. "Fundamentalists Launch Drive For Christian Voters." Washington Times (July 12, 1984).

530 Taylor, Paul. "Mississippi Christian School Pupils Give Hostile Reception to Mondale." Washington Post (September 14, 1984): A4.

531 Tsiantar, Dody. "Study Finds Jewish Vote Less Firm for Democrats." Washington Post (November 14, 1984).

532 Vorspan, Albert. "The Governor, the Archbishop, and the Jews." Reform Judaism 13 (Winter 1984-1985): 1, 32.

533 "Vote of Evangelicals in 1984." Emerging Trends 6 (December 1984): 6.

534 Wallis, Jim. "The President's Pulpit: A Look At Ronald Reagan's Theology." Sojourners 13 (September 1984): 17-21.

535 Wead, Doug and Bill. Reagan in Pursuit of the Presidency. Plainfield, N.J.: Haven Books, 1980.

536 Weinraub, Bernard. "Mondale Intends to Rebut Reagan on Religion Issue." New York Times (August 30, 1984): 1.

537 Weisman, Steven R. "Roman Catholic Shrine Is Site For Reagan Rally." New York Times (September 10, 1984): 1.

538 Whelan, Frank. "Religious Bigotry Has Been One Of America's Crosses To Bear." Allentown Morning Call (September 24, 1984): D1, D2.

539 Wicker, Tom. "The Ugliest Campaign." New York Times (October 19, 1984): A35.

540 Williams, Juan. "Bush Hits Religion Controversy." Washington Post (September 15, 1984): A7.

FRANKLIN D. ROOSEVELT

Franklin D. Roosevelt was a rather easygoing Episcopalian who seemed to enjoy his ancestral faith and to be somewhat interested in religious issues. He was also respectful of other religious traditions. Eleanor Roosevelt called his faith "simple and direct."

His churchgoing activities were fairly quiet and low-key, though a couple of anecdotes are worthy of note. One Easter FDR read the Episcopal service from the Book of Common Prayer to sailors aboard a ship in Key West. At Christmas of 1941, FDR took British Prime Minister Winston Churchill to a Methodist service to hear the lusty hymn-singing. Then they worshipped together at Christ Church in Alexandria, Virginia, George Washington's parish.

Roosevelt's foreign policies were controversial and somewhat unpopular among Catholic conservatives who disliked his recognition of Soviet Russia and his policies toward Spain and Mexico. Father Coughlin's extreme-right critiques of the New Deal won some Catholic support. (See Flynn, Shenton and Tull.)

Roosevelt's appointment of Myron Taylor as his personal representative to Pope Pius XII unleashed a torrent of Protestant criticism. (See Karmarkovic and Ken.) The Klingbeil dissertation is the best source for all of the church-state issues that arose during the Roosevelt Presidency.

The memoir from FDR's Labor Secretary Frances Perkins, the first woman cabinet member in U.S. history, includes a chapter on FDR's personal faith which is probably the best source of information on the subject.

See Bonnell, item 3, pp. 206-209.

See Fuller, item 8, pp. 201-206.

See Isely, item 12, pp. 243-248.

541 Flynn, George Q. American Catholics and the Roosevelt Presidency, 1932-1936. Lexington: University Press of Kentucky, 1968.

542 ------. Roosevelt and Romanism: Catholics and American Diplomacy. Westport: Greenwood Press, 1976.

543 Karmarkovic, Alex. "The Myron C. Taylor Appointment." Ph.D. dissertation. University of Minnesota, 1967.

544 Ken, William Aloysius. "American Involvement with the Vatican as a Moral Force in International Politics, 1939-1945." Ph.D. dissertation. Florida State University, 1975.

545 Kleiman, Max, ed. Roosevelt, the Tribute of the Synagogue. New York: Bloch Publishing, 1946.

546 Klingbeil, Kurt A. "F.D.R. and American Religious Leaders: A Study of President Franklin D. Roosevelt and His Relationship to Selected American Religious Leaders." Ph.D. dissertation. New York University, 1972.

547 Lachman, Seymour P. "The Cardinal, the Congressman and the First Lady." Journal of Church and State 7 (Winter 1965): 35-66.

548 "Methodists Assail Roosevelt." Literary Digest 119 (February 16, 1935): 17.

549 "Mr. Roosevelt's Sermon in Detroit." Christian Century 49 (October 12, 1932): 1229.

550 Perkins, Frances. The Roosevelt I Knew. New York: Viking, 1946. pp. 139-149.

551 "President's Letter Splits Clergy." Literary Digest 120 (October 5, 1935): 9.

552 "Priests Explain President's Notre Dame Degree." Newsweek 6 (December 14, 1935): 28.

553 Shenton, James P. "The Coughlin Movement and the New Deal." Political Science Quarterly 73 (1958): 352-373.

554 Tull, Charles J. Father Coughlin and the New Deal. Syracuse: Syracuse University Press, 1965.

555 Wartime Correspondence Between President Roosevelt and
    Pope Pius XII. New York: Macmillan, 1947.

THEODORE ROOSEVELT

Our vigorous and vital "Rough Rider" president was also the president of the "bully pulpit" and the "big stick." One of two Dutch Reformed presidents, he also attended the Episcopal Church (the church of his wife and children) so regularly that he could be considered dually-aligned.

Christian Reisner's book-length study, Roosevelt's Religion, is clearly the best source for this president's religious opinions. It is comprehensive, factual and anecdotal, even if it tends to see Roosevelt as perhaps a bit more religious than he was.

Though Roosevelt saw religion as part of an educated person's duty, he was somewhat skeptical of dogma and doctrine, or at least somewhat uninterested in theology. He saw religion as practical and pragmatic and, hence, was dismayed by conflicts among Christian groups over obscure doctrinal points. Reisner concluded, "Religion was the heart of his life, the creator of his ideals, the sustainer of his courage, the feeder of his faith, and the fountain of his wisdom. Without religion the greatness of Mr. Roosevelt is inexplicable."

Still, he knew enough about theology and the Bible to lecture at a seminary in California about the Bible, the only president to do so. He often gave a Christmas sermon at Christ Church in Oyster Bay, New York. He also taught Sunday School while he was a student at Harvard.

Roosevelt was a strong advocate of separation of church and state. (See article by Menendez) His opposition to religious intolerance and his appointment of Catholics and Jews to his Cabinet and to the Supreme Court were controversial among evangelical Protestants. For an interesting perspective, see Oscar Straus's article in Forum. Straus was the nation's first Jewish Cabinet member, appointed Secretary of Labor by Roosevelt.

Roosevelt's policies toward Catholicism, American Catholics and the Vatican are explored in an excellent book and two articles by a priest, Frederick Zwierlein. See also Mary Stuart's master's thesis.

See Bonnell, item 3, pp. 166-171.

See Fuller, item 8, pp. 162-168.

See Hampton, V., item 10, pp. 257-258; pp. 362-368.

See Hampton, W., item 11, pp. 79-86.

See Isely, item 12, pp. 195-200.

556 Menendez, Albert J. "Theodore Roosevelt on Church and State." Church & State 32 (July-August 1979): 14-16.

557 "Mr. Roosevelt's Religion." Literary Digest 63 (October 18, 1919): 30-31.

558 "Objections to the President's Letter on Religious Tolerance." Current Literature 46 (January 1909): 68-70.

559 "Our Preacher President." Independent 61 (December 13, 1906): 1431-1432.

560 "President Roosevelt's Address at the Presbyterian Assembly." Missionary Review of the World 25 (July 192): 533.

561 Reisner, Christian F. Roosevelt's Religion. New York: Abingdon, 1922.

562 Roosevelt, Theodore. "Shall We Do Away With the Church?" Ladies Home Journal 34 (October 1917): 12, 119.

563 Steiner, Franklin. The Religious Beliefs of Our Presidents. Girard, Ks.: Haldeman-Julius, 1936. pp. 152-156.

564 Straus, Oscar S. "The Religion of Roosevelt." Forum 69 (February 1923): 1191-1197.

565 Stuart, Mary Mauricita. "The Religious Convictions of Theodore Roosevelt and His Relations with Catholics and the Catholic Church." M.A. thesis. University of San Francisco, 1959.

566 "Theodore Roosevelt and Archbishop Ireland." Independent 54 (September 25, 1902): 2321-2323.

567 "Theodore Roosevelt's Religion." Current Opinion 72 (January 1922): 82-83.

568 "Theodore Roosevelt's Thanksgiving Proclamation, 1906." Independent 61 (November 1, 1906): 1015-1016.

569 Zwierlein, Frederick J. Theodore Roosevelt and Catholics 1882-1919. Rochester: Art Print Shop, 1956.

570 ------. Theodore Roosevelt and Catholics. St. Louis: Central Verein, 1956.

571 ------. "Theodore Roosevelt and Catholics." Social Justice Review 48 (1955): 60-64, 96-99, 150-155.

WILLIAM H. TAFT

William Howard Taft was a Unitarian whose religious views became an ugly issue in the 1908 election. Numerous fundamentalist and evangelical pastors urged Taft's defeat on religious grounds.

Taft was a firm Unitarian in conviction. He turned down the presidency of Yale University because he felt his religious beliefs were incompatible with the Congregationalist tradition then regnant at Old Eli.

He was an exceedingly tolerant man whose breadth of concern extended to people of all faiths. He held a particular concern for Jews, who were objects of persecution almost everywhere. Toward Catholics he was cordial and fairminded. As civil governor of the Philippines, he concluded a controversial treaty with the Vatican over some disputed friar's lands after the U.S. annexed the territory following the Spanish-American War. He also attended the Thanksgiving Day "Field Mass" during his Presidency. For those two abominable acts, he was condemned by many Protestants as a "friend of Popery." Charges of pro-Catholicism, as well as hatred for his Unitarian faith, plagued his campaign, but he still defeated William Jennings Bryan. (Taft's friend and mentor Theodore Roosevelt was incensed by the religious prejudice in the 1908 campaign and did what he could to counteract it.)

Taft's wife was an Episcopalian. His brother Charles was a prominent Presbyterian layman. His father, Judge Alphonso Taft, had been a Baptist but became a Unitarian.

On numerous occasions, Taft praised Christianity as a force for democracy and progress in the world.

An unsigned Nation magazine article and the article by Hornig are good sources for the 1908 election. The Taft-Catholic connection can be studied properly in Farrell, Goss, Reuter and Vivian.

See Bonnell, item 3, pp. 174-177.

See Fuller, item 8, pp. 169-173.

See Hampton, V., item 10, pp. 259-264.

See Hampton W., item 11, p. 87.

See Isely, item 12, pp. 203-208.

572 Farrell, J.T. "Background of the 1902 Taft Mission to Rome." Catholic Historical Review 36 (April 1950): 1-32; 37 (April 1951): 1-22.

573 Goss, E.F. "The Taft Commission to the Vatican, 1902." American Catholic History 46 (December 1936): 184-201.

574 Hornig, Edgar A. "The Religious Issue in the Taft-Bryan Duel of 1908." Proceedings of the American Philosophical Society 105 (1961): 530-537.

575 Reuter, Frank T. "William Howard Taft and the Separation of Church and State in the Philippines." Journal of Church and State 24 (Winter 1982): 105-117.

576 "Taft and his Religion." Nation 88 (February 8, 1908): 297-300.

577 Taft, William Howard. "Progressive World Struggle of the Jews for Civil Equality." National Geographic Magazine 36 (July 1919): 1-23.

578 Vivian, James F. "The Pan American Mass, 1909-1914: A Rejected Contribution to Thanksgiving Day." Church History 51 (September 1982): 321-333.

ZACHARY TAYLOR

With Zachary Taylor, we draw a zero on religious matters. A military career man, he seems to have had no interest in religion, save for an occasional visit to an Episcopal Church to please his wife, who was exceptionally devout. Taylor's daughter, though, claimed that he was "a constant reader of the Bible and practiced all its precepts." Still, he never joined any church.

There is some conflict concerning his funeral rite. (Taylor died in office after only sixteen months on the job.) Some historians say he is the only president who was buried without an "official" funeral celebration, but Edmund Fuller and David Green maintain that the Episcopal Burial Office was read at the White House.

Taylor was neither popular nor missed. Mormon leader Brigham Young said, "Zachary Taylor is dead and gone to hell, and I am glad of it."

See Bonnell, item 3, pp. 86-89.

See Fuller, item 8, pp. 87-88.

See Hampton, V., item 10, pp. 218-220.

See Hampton, W., item 11, p. 43.

See Isely, item 12, pp. 91-96.

HARRY TRUMAN

Harry Truman was a delightfully outspoken Missouri Baptist who delighted in ridiculing his co-religionists when he thought they were being petty or bigoted. He detested clerics who meddled in politics and once severed his connection with Washington's First Baptist Church after the pastor denounced his attempt to initiate diplomatic exchanges with the Vatican (while Truman was present, no less!) He told the press that he "cussed out the Baptists" down South during the 1960 Presidential campaign when so many clergy were urging their flock to vote against a Catholic president.

Truman had deep religious convictions and knew the Scriptures well, but, like Kennedy, he considered religion, ethics and morality private matters. But he did indulge in religious invocations on ceremonial occasions and once wished the "blessings of the Holy Spirit" on Americans during the Christmas season.

His wife and daughter were Episcopalians. An interesting chapter could be written on another phenomenon of presidential religion: the unusually large number of Episcopalian wives of non-Episcopalian presidents, including Truman, Lyndon Johnson, Taft, Arthur, Teddy Roosevelt, Taylor and Wilson (his second wife).

Truman's major church-state problem was the Vatican Ambassador question, when a "Protestant Typhoon" forced him to withdraw the nomination of General Mark Clark as U.S. Ambassador-designate to the Holy See.

See Gustafson for insights into Truman's religion and its influence on his policies. Bickerton, Cohen and Snetsinger concentrate on Truman's relationships with the Jewish community and with Israel. His problems with Protestants during the Vatican Ambassador controversy are described by Deaton and by articles in the popular Catholic and Protestant press. Reverend Edward H. Pruden remembers his conflict with Truman in <u>A Window On Washington</u>.

See Bonnell, item 3, pp. 212-215.

See Fuller, item 8, pp. 207-215.

See Isely, item 12, pp. 251-256.

579 "Argonaut's Sane Comments: the Exchange of Letters by the Pope and the President." Ave Maria 66 (September 27, 1947): 386-387.

580 "Baptist on Brotherhood." Time 63 (April 12, 1954): 85.

581 Bickerton, Ian. "President Truman's Recognition of Israel." American Jewish Historical Quarterly 58 (December 1968): 173-240.

582 Cohen, Michael J. "Truman and Palestine, 1945-1948: Revisionism, Politics and Diplomacy." Modern Judaism 2 (February 1982): 1-22.

583 "Christmas Eve Talk, December 24, 1948." Catholic Mind 47 (March 1949): 19-192.

584 "Correspondence between President Truman and Pope Pius XII." Catholic Mind 51 (October 1953): 625-640.

585 Deaton, Dorsey M. "The Protestant Crisis: Truman's Vatican Ambassador Crisis of 1951." Ph.D. dissertation. Emory University, 1969.

586 "Former President Truman Lauds Integrated Catholic Hospital." Interracial Review 28 (June 1955): 105.

587 Gustafson, Merlin. "Church, State and the Cold War, 1945-1952." Journal of Church and State 8 (Winter 1966): 49-63.

588 ------. "The Church, the State, and the Military in the Truman Administration." Rocky Mountain Social Science Journal 2 (October 1965): 2-10.

589 ------. "Religion and Politics in the Truman Administration." Rocky Mountain Social Science Journal 3 (October 1966): 125-134.

590 ------. "Religion of a President." Journal of Church and State 10 (Autumn 1968): 379-387.

591 ------. "Harry Truman as a Man of Faith." Christian Century 90 (January 17, 1973): 75-78.

592 "Holy See Sends Message." Ave Maria 72 (December 2, 1950): 706.

593 "Investigating the Clergy; Question Raised by Former President Truman." America 90 (November 28, 1953): 217.

594 "Letters Exchanged between President Truman and Pope Pius XII." Catholic Mind 45 (November 1947): 651-655.

595 "Letters of President Truman to the Holy Father, December 17, 1949 and the Pontiff's Reply." Catholic Mind 48 (February 1950): 125-127.

596 "Mr. Taylor to the Vatican." Catholic Mind 44 (July 1946): 444.

597 "Mr. Truman and Pius XII." America 89 (May 9, 1953): 154.

598 "Mr. Truman Attends Sunday School." Christian Century 64 (October 15, 1945): 1228.

599 "Pius XII receives Truman." America 95 (June 2, 1956): 236.

600 "Pope Pius XII and President Truman; an exchange of letters." Tablet 190 (September 6, 1947): 151-152.

601 "President on the Meaning of Christmas." America 82 (January 7, 1950): 402-403.

602 "President and Pope." America 77 (September 13, 1947): 650.

603 "President Prays." Life 29 (July 10, 1950): 32.

604 "President surrenders to the Pope." Christian Century 68 (October 31, 1951): 1243-1244.

605 "President to the Pope; message, December 17th, 1949." Tablet 194 (December 31, 1949): 473.

606 "President's Christian Message on Good Friday." Ave Maria 73 (April 14, 1951): 452.

607 Pruden, Edward Hughes. "Mr. Truman Comes to Church" in A Window on Washington. New York: Vantage Press, 1976. pp. 41-105.

608 "Religion and Brotherhood; Address to the NCCJ November 11, 1949." Catholic Mind 48 (January 1950): 61-64.

609 Snetsinger, John. Truman, The Jewish Vote, and the Creation of Israel. Stanford, Ca.: Hoover Institution Press, 1974.

610 Truman, Harry. "Greetings to Catholic Library Association." Catholic Library World 22 (October 1950): 4.

611 ------. "In God We Trust; Address, September 28, 1951." Catholic Mind 50 (May 1952): 263-267.

612 "Why did he do it? [Ambassador to the Vatican]." Christian Century 68 (November 7, 1951): 1269-1671.

JOHN TYLER

Tyler was the fifth Virginia Episcopalian to serve in the Presidency. Typical of his heritage, he was undemonstrative in religious practices and habits. He rarely alluded to religion and kept ceremonial religious utterances to a minimum.

But his religious activities always took place in Episcopal churches. His second marriage was solemnized by the bishop of New York. He was also quite familiar with the Bible.

His second wife, Julia Gardiner Tyler, became a convert to Catholicism some years after his death. She was devoted to her new faith and practiced it with considerable fervor.

Very little has been written about his religious life.

See Bonnell, item 3, pp. 74-77.

See Fuller, item 8, pp. 77-80.

See Hampton, V., item 10, pp. 215-218.

See Isely, item 12, pp. 75-80.

613 Seager, Robert II. And Tyler Too: A Biography of John and Julia Gardiner Tyler. New York: McGraw-Hill, 1963.

MARTIN VAN BUREN

Martin Van Buren was the first Dutch Reformed president. A consummate New York politician, Van Buren accepted his ancestral faith and always attended church. Religion remained an integral part of his life, but he showed no intellectual curiosity about theology.

Since there was no Dutch Reformed church in Washington, Van Buren attended St. John's Episcopal Church and even held a pew there--a remarkable similarity to another New Yorker, Theodore Roosevelt, who also attended both the Reformed and Episcopal Churches. His 1862 funeral service was jointly conducted by a Reformed pastor and the Episcopal bishop of Pennsylvania, a close friend.

Not much has been written about his religious life.

See Bonnell, item 3, pp. 62-65.

See Fuller, item 8, pp. 68-72.

See Hampton, V., item 10, pp. 213-214; pp. 359-362.

See Isely, item 12, pp. 59-64.

GEORGE WASHINGTON

Our first President's religious views have been the subject of considerable debate. Religious conservatives have tried to stress his personal piety and belief in Providence. Washington's frequent references to the interrelationship between religion, morality and democracy have been cited as evidence of his adherence to orthodoxy. See Johnstone, Sprague, Brustat, and Littell.

Many religious liberals and humanists have tried to claim Washington's reticence to discuss dogma or doctrine as evidence of a kind of eighteenth-century deism. See Remsburg and Steiner.

Episcopalian scholars stress Washington's life-long commitment to church and vestry membership. See Brinker, Buckley, Humphreys, Kinsolving, Sydnor, and Tucker. Religious libertarians cite his strong support for religious liberty and the First Amendment. See Barnes and Menendez.

So it is easy to agree with this assertion of Paul F. Boller, Jr.: "Perhaps nothing about Washington has been so thoroughly clouded by myth, legend, misunderstanding and misrepresentation as his religious outlook." Boller continues, "When it comes to Washington's religion, professional historians and biographers writing in the twentieth century have tended either to pass over the subject in silence, to classify Washington with Franklin, Jefferson, and Paine, and then pass on to another topic, or to describe only the more obvious aspects of Washington's religious behavior. The field has thus been left largely to writers with "parti pris." Historians with sectarian attachments have been eager to emphasize—and they inevitably exaggerate—the extent of Washington's associations with and partiality for their particular denominations. Evangelical writers and filiopietists have busily accumulated pious fables about Washington's religious habits whose historicity many Americans today still regard as unquestioned. Militant secularists, on the other hand, have been so preoccupied with the useful and necessary work of exploding the myths about Washington that they have had neither the time nor the inclination to inquire into the actualities of Washington's religious life. Their uniform assumption, however, is that whatever Washington may have said in public, he was, at heart, an anticlerical."

Boller's book, George Washington and Religion, written to counteract the propagandistic writings he deplored, is by far the best source for information about Washington's involvement with the Episcopal church, his respect for other religious communities and his unswerving commitment to religious liberty. An appendix includes Washington's major religious statements.

Washington's cordial relationship with the Roman Catholic and Jewish communities can be ascertained in Abraham, Carne, Clarke, Lewis, and Ulmann.

Note, also, that the U.S. George Washington Bicentennial Commission published a compilation of Washington's religious references in 1931.

See Bonnell, item 3, pp. 18-24.

See Fuller, item 8, pp. 8-17.

See Hampton, V., item 10, pp. 196-199; pp. 330-337.

See Hampton, W., item 11, pp. 12-15.

See Isely, item 12, pp. 3-8.

614 Abraham, Lewis. "Correspondence Between Washington and Jewish Citizens." Proceedings of the American Jewish Historical Society 3 (1894): 87-96.

615 Bailey, Olive D. Christmas with the Washingtons. Richmond: Dietz Press, 1948.

616 Barnes, Lemuel C. "George Washington and Freedom of Conscience." Journal of Religion 12 (October 1932): 493-525.

617 Beatty, Albert R. "Was Washington Religious?" National Republic 20 (February 1933): 3-5, 28; 20 (March 1933): 18-19, 29.

618 Boller, Paul F., Jr. George Washington and Religion. Dallas: Southern Methodist University Press, 1963.

619 ------. "George Washington and the Methodists." Historical Magazine of the Protestant Episcopal Church 27 (June 1959): 165-86.

620 ------. "George Washington and the Presbyterians." Journal of the Presbyterian Historical Society 39 (September 1961): 129-149.

621 ------. "George Washington and the Quakers." Bulletin of Friends Historical Association 49 (Autumn 1960): 67-83.

622 Brinker, Evva. "George Washington the Vestryman and His Services as a Churchman." Picket Post (April 1948): 14-16.

623 Brustat, A.W. "Washington, Christian Patriot." American Mercury 80 (1955): 125-127.

624 Buckley, James M. "Washington as a Christian and a Communicant." Independent 50 (February 17, 1898): 205-207; 50 (February 24, 1898): 240-241.

625 Buffington, Joseph. The Soul of Washington. Philadelphia: Dorrance and Company, 1936.

626 Carne, W.F. "George Washington and the Church." Catholic World 30 (1880): 491.

627 "Catholicity and Washington." American Catholic Historical Researches 19 (192): 55.

628 Clarke, Richard H. "George Washington in His Relations with Catholics." American Catholic Quarterly Review 21 (1896): 636-656.

629 ------. "George Washington." American Catholic Quarterly Review 21 (1896): 250+.

630 Conrad, Frederick W. "Washington: Christianity and the Moulding Power of His Character." Lutheran Quarterly 26 (1896): 89-115.

631 Conway, Moncure D. "George Washington and Reverend Jonathan Boucher." Lippincott's Magazine 43 (1892): 722.

632 ------. "The Religion of George Washington." Open Court 3 (October 24, 1889).

633 Cousins, Norman, ed. In God We Trust. New York: Harper, 1958. pp. 44-73.

634 Davis, Edwin. "The Religion of George Washington: A Bicentennial Report." Air University Review 27 (1976): 30-34.

635 Demarest, William H.S. "George Washington's Religion." Huguenot (May 1932): 1, 12.

636 Dunlap, Edward Slater. George Washington as a Christian and Churchman. Washington, D.C.: Cathedral of St. Peter and St. Paul, 1932.

637 "First Thanksgiving Proclamation, 1789." Journal of Education 68 (1908): 520.

638 Fleming, T. "Washington's Prayer at Valley Forge." Reader's Digest 104 (1974): 110-112.

639 Flexner, J.T. "The Miraculous Care of Providence." American Heritage 33 (1982): 82-85.

640 "George Washington and Archbishop Carroll." American Catholic Historical Researches 17 (1900): 49-52.

641 Hamilton, Mrs. Alexander. Witness That George Washington Was a Communicant of the Church. Hartford: Church Missions Publishing Company, 1932.

642 Harris, Carlton D. "Was Washington a Christian or Profane, Irreligious and Worldly-Minded?" Minute Man 21 (June 1926): 83-87.

643 Humphreys, Francis Landon. George Washington, the Churchman. Palm Beach: 1932.

644 "Items Relating to Correspondence of Jews with George Washington." Publications of the American Jewish Historical Society 27 (1920): 217-222.

645 Johnstone, William J. George Washington the Christian. Cincinnati: Abingdon Press, 1919.

646 ------. How Washington Prayed. New York: Abingdon Press, 1932.

647 Kinsolving, Arthur B. "The Religion of George Washington." *Historical Magazine of the Protestant Episcopal Church* 18 (September 1949): 326-332.

648 Kremer, A.H. "The Religious Character of Washington." *Mercersburg Review* 11 (1859): 211-222.

649 Lewis, Abraham. *Correspondence Between Washington and Jewish Citizens*. Baltimore: The Friedenwald Company, 1895.

650 Littell, Rev. John Stockton. *Washington: Christian*. Keene, N.H.: Hampshire Art Press, 1913.

651 Marty, Martin E. "Washington on his Knees; A Pamphlet Writer's Myth." *Christian Century* 90 (1973): 327.

652 McCabe, L. R. "Washington's Reverence." *Saint Nicholas* 31 (1902): 318-319.

653 McComas, Joseph Patton. "Washington—the Churchman in New York." *Huguenot* (February 1932): 4+.

654 McGuire, Edward C. *The Religious Opinions and Character of Washington*. New York: Harper and Brothers, 1836.

655 Menendez, Albert J. "George Washington and Religious Liberty." *Church & State* 31 (December 1978): 14-16.

656 Nash, J.V. "The Religion and Philosophy of Washington." *Open Court* 43 (February 1932): 73-92.

657 Oldham, G. Ashton. "Washington, Christian Statesman." *Holiletic Review* 95 (February 1928): 144-146.

658 Perry, W.S. "Religious Character of George Washington." *Christian Literature* 10 (1895): 53.

659 Porter, Frank G. "Washington as Bishop Asbury Saw Him." *Methodist Review* 93 (July 1930): 513-521.

660 Remsburg, John E. *Six Historic Americans*. New York: The Truth Seeker Company, 1906. pp. 101-149.

661 Smylie, James H. "The President as Republican Prophet and King: Clerical Reflections on the Death of Washington." *Journal of Church and State* 18 (Spring 1976): 233-252.

662 Sprague, Frederick W. Washington, the One in Prophecy Like the Son of Man. Newport, R.I.: 1873.

663 Steiner, Franklin. The Religious Beliefs of Our Presidents. Girard, Ks.: Haldeman-Julius, 1936. pp. 14-41, 160-172.

664 ------. "That Alleged Prayer of G. Washington." Truth Seeker 54 (July 28, 1927): 474-475.

665 ------. "That Washington Prayer Again." Truth Seeker 59 (December 31, 1927): 842.

666 Stone, William L. "Was Washington a Christian?" Magazine of American History 13 (June 1885): 596-597.

667 Sydnor, William. "George Washington's Connection with Christ Church, Alexandria, Virginia." Historical Magazine of the Protestant Episcopal Church 45 (1976): 110-111.

668 Taylor, Malcolm. "Washington as a Christian." Magazine of History 22 (1915): 88-93.

669 Tucker, Reverend Beverly. "Washington as a Churchman." Churchman 78 (October 8, 1898).

670 Ulmann, Albert. "George Washington and the Jews." Judean Addresses 4 (1933): 202-211.

671 Vernon, Merle. Washington: The Soldier and the Christian. New York: Military Post Library Association.

672 "Washington as a Communicant of the Church: Testimony of an Eye-Witness to Washington's Frequent Communions While President." Churchman 79 (1899): 795-798.

673 "Washington at the Communion Table in Morristown, New Jersey." Presbyterian Magazine 1 (December 1851): 569-571.

674 Washington, George. Religious References in the Writings, Addresses, and Military Orders of George Washington. Washington, D.C.: The United States George Washington Bicentennial Commission, 1931.

675 Whittekin, W.H. "George Never So Prayed." *Truth Seeker* 56 (July 27, 1929): 474.

WOODROW WILSON

Wilson, a Presbyterian pastor's son, brought his scholarly, critical mind to bear on religious matters as well as secular ones. His preeminent biographer Arthur S. Link suggested that Wilson's policies could not be understood except in light of his evangelical Presbyterian faith and its emphasis on order, reason and righteousness.

Link wrote, "Woodrow Wilson stands pre-eminent among all the inheritors of the Calvinist tradition who have made significant contributions to American political history. Indeed, he was the prime embodiment, the apogee, of the Calvinist tradition among statesmen of the modern epoch. Every biographer of Wilson has said that it is impossible to know and understand the man apart from his religious faith. His every action and policy was ultimately informed and molded by the Christian insight that it was given him to have."

Wilson's now-forgotten sermons at Princeton University have been rediscovered and analyzed by John Mulder.

Wilson's close personal friend and physician, Admiral Cary Grayson, tells a good deal about Wilson's personal religious habits and beliefs in a memoir published almost 40 years after the President's death. Wilson's own article in Century magazine gives some revealing insights.

Wilson had some problems with Catholic voters. Though he was a Democrat, a party which traditionally relied on Catholic support to win elections, Wilson appointed no Catholics to his Cabinet or to the Supreme Court during two full terms of office. This was strange and seemingly insensitive, especially since his three Republican predecessors had done so. And the Republican Party did not rely much on Catholic support in those days. This was a major source of unhappiness. So was Wilson's policy toward anticlerical governments in Mexico and his strained relations with the Vatican over the conduct of World War I and postwar reconstruction. (See Bucher, Leary, Mullen and Zivojinovic.)

Still, when Wilson did appoint a Catholic, Joseph Tumulty, as his private secretary--a position more important than today and roughly comparable to the White House Chief of Staff—Protestant opinion was outraged. Tumulty was called a Vatican spy. See his volume of memoirs and Blum's admirable study.

Wilson's own personal interest in missionaries and related matters is studied in Soper, Taylor and Trani.

Wilson as a moralist is considered by Bishirjian and Handlin.

See Bonnell, item 3, pp. 180-185.

See Fuller, item 8, pp. 174-183.

See Hampton, V., item 10, pp. 90-101.

See Hampton, W., item 11, pp. 88-90.

See Isely, item 12, pp. 211-216.

676 Bishirjian, Richard T. "Croly, Wilson, and the American Civil Religion." Modern Age 23 (1979): 33-38.

677 Blum, John M. Joe Tumulty and the Wilson Era. Boston: Houghton Mifflin, 1951.

678 Bucher, Betty R. "Catholics and Woodrow Wilson's Mexican Policy." M.A. thesis. Catholic University of America, 1954.

679 Grayson, Cary. Woodrow Wilson: An Intimate Memoir. New York: Holt, Rinehart, & Winston, 1960.

680 Handlin, Oscar, ed. Woodrow Wilson and the Politics of Morality. Boston: Little, Brown, and Company, 1956.

681 "Jewish Favor for Mr. Wilson." Literary Digest 54 (1917): 24.

682 Leary, W.M., Jr. "Woodrow Wilson, Irish-Americans and the Elections of 1916." Journal of American History 54 (1967): 57-72.

683 Link, Arthur S. "Woodrow Wilson: Christian in Government." Christianity Today 8 (July 3, 1964): 6-10.

684 "Mr. Wilson's Catholic Critics." Literary Digest 51 (1915): 1481-1482.

685 Mulder, John M. "Wilson the Preacher." Journal of Presbyterian History 51 (Fall 1973): 267-284.

686 Mullen, Sister Francis Charles. "Catholic Attitudes Towards Woodrow Wilson." M.A. thesis. Boston College, 1960.

687 "The President on Religious Education." Literary Digest 48 (1914): 1438-1439.

688 "President Wilson and Others Seek to Revitalize the Country Church." Current Opinion 60 (1916): 112-113.

689 "President's Proclamation Asks Prayers for Peace." Journal of Education 80 (1914): 231.

690 "Religious Utterances of the President-Elect." Literary Digest 45 (1912): 1067-1068.

691 Soper, David Wesley. "Woodrow Wilson and the Christian Tradition." Ph.D. dissertation. Drew University, 1945.

692 Taylor, James Henry. Woodrow Wilson in Church, his Membership in the Congregation of the Central Presbyterian Church, Washington, D.C., 1913-1924. Charleston, S.C.: J.H. Taylor, 1952.

693 Trani, Eugene P. "Woodrow Wilson, China, and the Missionaries, 1913-1921." Journal of Presbyterian History 49 (1971): 328-351.

694 Tumulty, Joseph. Woodrow Wilson As I Know Him. New York: Literary Digest, 1921.

695 Wilson, Woodrow. "When a Man Comes to Himself." Century 50 (June 1901): 268-273.

696 Zivojinovic, Dragan R. The United States and the Vatican Policies, 1914-1918. Boulder: Colorado Associated University Press, 1978.

AUTHOR INDEX

Abbott, Lyman 281-282
Abraham, Lewis 614
Abram, Morris B. 45
Adams, Dickinson Ward 182
Adams, John Quincy 32-37
Adler, Cyrus 183
Agar, Herbert 105
Alley, Robert S. 1, 380
Anderson, John R. 184

Bailey, Olive D. 615
Baker, E.G. 38
Baker, James T. 46-47
Banks, Louis Albert 39, 152, 160, 174, 283, 386
Barnes, Lemuel C. 616
Barrett, Patricia 258
Barton, Bruce 284
Barton, Frederick 387
Barton, William E. 285
Bates, William H. 286
Bauer, Gerald 185
Beardslee, C.S. 287
Beatty, Albert R. 617
Bennett, H. Omer 186
Bickerton, Ian 581
Bird, John 251
Bishirjian, Richard T. 676
Blied, Benjamin J. 288
Blum, John M. 677
Blumenthal, Sidney 421
Bole, William 422
Boller, Paul F., Jr. 2, 618-621
Bonnell, John Sutherland 3
Brant, Irving 381
Brent, Robert A. 187
Briggs, Kenneth A. 48
Briggs, Linda L. 259

Brinker, Evva 622
Brown, Barbara 188
Brownlow, John R. 250
Brustat, A.W. 623
Brydon, G. Maclaren 189
Bucher, Betty R. 678
Buckley, James M. 624
Buckley, Thomas E. 190
Buffington, Joseph 625
Buie, James 423-425
Bullard, F. Lauriston 289

Carey, Joseph 426
Carne, W.F. 626
Carter, Jimmy 51
Castelli, Jim 54, 427
Chandler, Russell 391
Chesterton, G.K. 162
Chittenden, L.E. 290
Christian, John T. 191
Clancy, T.H. 291
Clapp, Rodney 428
Clark, Bayard S. 292
Clarke, Richard H. 628-629
Clendinen, Dudley 429
Clymer, Adam 430
Coffin, T.E. 390
Cohen, Michael J. 582
Coleman, Milton 431
Collis, Charles H.T. 293
Collum, Danny 432-434
Conn, Joseph 435-438
Conrad, Frederick W. 630
Converse, Phillip E. 262
Conway, Moncure D. 631-632
Costanzo, Joseph F. 192
Cousins, Norman 29, 193, 382, 633
Crawford, Nelson Antrim 194

135

Crismon, L.T. 295
Cronkhite, L.G. 294
Crothers, Samuel McChord 195
Cuomo, Mario 439

Dahl, Curtis 175
Davis, Edwin 634
Davis, Thurston N. 196
Dawidowicz, Lucy 440
Deaton, Dorsey M. 585
DeCleyre, Voltairine 296
Demarest, William H.S. 635
DeWitt, John 441
Dickenson, James R. 442-444
DiVeroli, Robert 445-446
Donahue, Bernard F. 394
Douglas, Bruce 57
Doyle, Barrie 147, 395
Drakeman, Donald L. 383
Drinan, Robert F. 58
Droel, William M. 447
Drouin, Edmond G. 197
D'Souza, Dinesh 448
Dugan, Robert P., Jr. 449
Dulce, Berton 4
Dunlap, Edward Slater 636
Dunnam, Spurgeon M., III 450

Eisenhower, Dwight D. 109-113, 117
Elbert, David 451
Eliot, Frederick May 198
Ellen, Vernard 252
Endy, Melvin B., Jr. 299
Erickson, Gary Lee 300
Erickson, Keith V. 59
Ericson, Edward L. 199
Everett, Robert B. 30

Fairbanks, James David 5, 452
Farnham, Wallace D. 6
Farrell, J.T. 572
Fesperman, Francis I. 200
Fish, C.R. 301
Fisher, Paul A. 453
Fiske, Edward 396
Fitch, Robert E. 116
Flamini, Roland 263
Fleming, T. 638

Flexner, J.T. 639
Flowers, Ronald B. 60
Flynn, George Q. 541-542
Foote, Henry Wilder 201
Forrest, W.M. 202
Fox, Frederic 7
Fox, Gresham George 302
Frawley, Joan 454-455
Freese, A.S. 61
Fritchman, Stephen Hole 203
Fuchs, Lawrence H. 264
Fuller, Edmund 8, 303

Gannett, E.S. 40
Gaver, Jessica Russell 62
Goldman, Ari L. 456
Good, Douglas 304
Goodspeed, Edgar J. 204
Goss, E.F. 573
Gordon, Max 457
Gould, William Drum 205-206
Grayson, Cary 679
Green, David E. 8, 303
Greenbie, Sydney and Marjorie 305
Grierson, Francis 306
Gummere, W. 163
Gurley, Phineas D. 307
Gustafson, Merlin 9, 118, 164, 587-591

Hall, J. Lesslie 207
Halliday, E.M. 208
Hamilton, Mrs. Alexander 641
Hamilton, J.G. de Roulhac 209
Hampton, Vernon B. 10
Hampton, William Judson 11
Hanchett, William 308
Handlin, Oscar 680
Hardon, John A. 210, 265
Harris, Carlton D. 642
Harris, Thomas M. 309
Hartnett, Robert C. 119
Hays, Charlotte 458
Healey, Robert M. 211
Hefley, James 64, 148
Henderson, Charles P. 398-399

Author Index

Hensel, William U. 42-43
Herbers, John 459-465
Hill, John Wesley 310
Himmelfarb, Milton 65
Hinshaw, David 166
Horn, Stanley F. 176
Horner, Harlan Hoyt 311
Hornig, Edgar A. 574
Horsley, Catherine Dunscombe 212
House, Albert V. 312
Howard, F. 313
Hoyt, Robert 266
Huffman, Kenneth 400
Hughes, Arthur J. 66
Humphreys, Francis 643
Hunt, Gaillard 213, 385
Huntley, William B. 214
Hurley, Doran 314
Hutcheson, R.G. 67
Hutchins, Robert Maynard 215
Hutchinson, Bob 466
Hutchinson, Paul 120
Hyer, Marjorie 467-468

Ingwerson, Marshall 469
Irwin, B.F. 315
Isely, Bliss 12

Jackson, John R. 316
Jackson, S. Trevana 317
James, E.S. 267
Jaroslovsky, Rich 470
Jefferson, Thomas 216
Johnson, Haynes 472
Johnstone, William J. 318-319, 645-646
Jones, Edgar DeWitt 218, 320
Jones, Olga 13
Jorstad, Erling 69
Joyce, Fay S. 473

Karmarkovic, Alex 543
Kay, Miryan Neulander 219
Keller, Robert H., Jr. 159
Kemper, Deane Alwyn 268
Ken, William Aloysius 544
Kilgo, John Carlisle 220
Kim, Richard C. 269

King, N. 70
Kinsolving, Arthur B. 221, 647
Kirby, J.E. 321
Kleiman, Max 545
Klein, Philip S. 44
Klingbeil, Kurt A. 546
Knoles, George Harmon 222
Kramer, Michael 402
Kremer, A.H. 648
Kristol, Irving 474
Kucharsky, David 14-15
Kuper, Theodore Fred 223
Kurzweil, John 475

Lachman, Seymour P. 547
LaFontaine, Charles V. 16
LaHaye, Tim 476
Landau, Yehezkel 477
Lane, T.A. 322
Langley, Lester D. 177
Landsdowne, Stuart 255
Leary, W.M., Jr. 682
Lefever, Ernest W. 123
Lewis, Abraham 649
Lewis, Joseph 323
Linder, Robert 478
Lindstrom, Ralph G. 325
Linhardt, Arnold 479
Link, Arthur S. 683
Lippy, Charles H. 326
Lipset, Seymour Martin 71, 480-481
Littell, Rev. John Stockton 650
Little, David 224-225
Locigno, J.P. 226
Logan, Thomas D. 327
Ludwig, Charles 328
Luebke, Fred C. 227-228
Lynch, John 329

Mabee, Charles 229
Macartney, Clarence 330
MacPherson, Myra 484
Macropoulos, Elias 270
Maddox, Robert L. 72
Maidens, Melinda 482
Malone, T.J. 331

Marty, Martin 651
Mather, P.B. 168
Mathews, A.H. 74
Matt, A.J., Jr. 485
Mayer, Milton 403
Maynard, Nettie Colburn 332
McCabe, Joseph 17
McCabe, L.R. 652
McCarty, Burke 333
McCollister, John 18, 334
McComas, Joseph Patton 653
McConagha, Alan 483
McCrie, George M. 335
McGuire, Edward C. 654
McKinley, William 388
McLoughlin, Emmett 336
McMurtrie, Douglas C. 337
McWilliams, Carey 404
Mead, Sidney E. 230, 338
Medhurst, Martin J. 19
Meehan, Thomas F. 339
Mehta, M.J. 231
Menendez, Albert J. 20-21, 75-76, 271-272, 486-490, 556, 655
Michener, James A. 273
Miller, Arthur H. 491
Miller, William Lee 77, 124-126
Mills, James 492
Moellering, Ralph 405
Moley, Ray 169
Mondale, Walter 494
Moody, Sid 495
Moore, Arthur 78
Morgenthau, Hans J. 340
Mott, Royden J. 232
Mouat, Lucia 496
Mulder, John M. 685
Mullen, Sister Francis Charles 686
Murphy, K. 79

Nadich, Judah 127
Nall, Stephanie 497
Nannes, Caspar 80, 128
Nash, J.V. 656
Neely, Matthew 129

Newton, Joseph Fort 233
Nicolay, John G. 342
Niebuhr, Reinhold 343
Nielson, Niels 81
Nixon, Richard M. 406
Noll, Mark A. 344
Norton, Howard 82
Novak, Michael 409

O'Brien, John C. 130
Odegard, Peter H. 22
Oldham, G. Ashton 657
Oliver, Henry 345
Oreskes, Michael 498
Osborne, John 83, 410
Owen, George Frederick 346

Parmlew, Helen 131
Parsons, Wilfrid Joe 170
Paschall, G. Spurgeon 234
Pearson, Samuel C. 235
Pennell, Orrin Henry 347
Perkins, Frances 550
Perry, James W. 499
Perry, W.S. 658
Peters, Madison C. 348
Pierard, Richard V. 23, 500-502
Pierce, Kenneth M. 503
Pike, James A. 274
Pippert, Wesley 84-86
Plochl, Willibald M. 236
Plowman, Edward E. 87-89, 132, 149
Porter, Frank G. 659
Powell, E.P. 237
Pressman, Steven 505
Pruden, Edward Hughes 607

Rager, John C. 238
Randall, Claire 90
Randall, J.G. 349
Randall, R.P. 350
Reagan, Ronald 506
Redlich, Norman 507
Reed, James A. 351
Reed, W.A. 91
Reeves, Richard 92

Author Index

Reeves, Robert N. 352
Reichley, A. James 508
Reisner, Christian F. 561
Remsburg, John Eleazer 239, 353, 660
Reston, James 509
Reuter, Frank T. 389, 575
Richelsen, John 172
Richmond, M.E.M. 93
Robbins, Peggy 354
Robertson, Nan 257
Robinson, L.E. 355
Rodden, John 510
Roger, R.C. 356
Rogers, David 511
Roosevelt, Theodore 562
Rose, William 512
Rowland, Kathleen 275
Rushford, Jerry Bryant 153

Saikowski, Charlotte 513
Salmans, Sandra 514
Sandler, S. Gerald 240
Sanford, Charles B. 241
Schaff, David S. 242
Schanberg, Sydney H. 515
Schlesinger, Arthur, Jr. 516
Schneider, Nicholas A. 276
Schneider, William 517
Schulz, Constance B. 31, 243
Schwartz, Michael 518
Seager, Robert II 613
Settel, T.S. 277
Settle, R.W. 357
Shea, John Gilmary 154
Shenton, James P. 553
Shepherd, David R. 519
Sievers, Harry J. 161
Simbro, William 520
Slosser, Bob 521
Smith, T.V. 358
Smylie, James H. 661
Sneed, J. Richard 103
Snetsinger, John 609
Sobran, Joseph 522-524
Soper, David Wesley 691
Speakman, Frederick B. 359
Sperry, Willard L. 360

Spoelstra, Watson 150
Sprague, Frederick W. 662
Spring, Beth 525-527
Stapleton, Ruth Carter 94
Star, John William 361
Stedman, Murray S. 24
Steiner, B.C. 178
Steiner, Franklin 25, 155, 563, 663-665
Stern, P.V. 362
Stern, Sol 528
Stickley, Julia Ward 179
Stone, William L. 666
Storer, J.W. 26
Stowe, Walter H. 244
Strachan, Jill Penelope 414
Straus, Oscar S. 564
Strobel, Warren 529
Stuart, Mary Mauricita 565
Sunderland, Byron 156
Swancara, Frank 245
Swomley, John M. 415
Sydnor, William 667

Taft, William Howard 577
Tansey, Ann 363
Tarbell, Ida 364
Taylor, James Henry 692
Taylor, Malcolm 668
Taylor, Paul 530
Tegeder, V.C. 365
Thayer, George A. 366
Thompson, D. 367
Toolin, Cynthia 27
Trainor, M. Rosaleen 246
Trani, Eugene P. 693
Trueblood, Elton 368
Truman, Harry 610-611
Tsiantar, Dody 531
Tucker, Reverend Beverly 669
Tull, Charles J. 554
Tumulty, Joseph 694
Tyler, B.B. 369

Ulmann, Albert 670

Vernon, Merle 671
Vivian, James F. 578

Vorspan, Albert 532

Walker, Arda 180
Walker, David Ellis, Jr. 278
Wall, James M. 95-97
Wallis, Jim 539
Wasson, Woodrow W. 157-158
Watson, Edward L. 370
Wead, Doug and Bill 540
Weil, Eric 146
Weinraub, Bernard 534
Weisman, Steven R. 535
Wells, Ronald A. 28
West, Earl Irvin 41, 181, 420
Wettstein, A. Arnold 247
Whelan, Frank 536
White, Kermit E. 371
Whitelaw, David P. 372
Whittekin, W.H. 675
Wicker, Tom 537
Wicks, Elliott K. 248
Wiest, Walter E. 373
Williams, Juan 538
Wills, Garry 416
Wilson, Edmund 374
Wilson, John R.M. 173
Wilson, Woodrow 695
Wimberly, Ronald C. 417
Winter, Don 98
Wolf, William J. 375-377
Wolfe, James Snow 279-280
Woods, R.L. 378
Woodward, Kenneth L. 418
Wright, James C. 379

Zeoli, Billy 151
Zivojinovic, Dragan R. 696
Zwierlein, Frederick J. 249, 569-571

SUBJECT INDEX

Abortion 55, 442, 466, 523
Armageddon 459, 465, 477, 492, 520

Baptists 46-47, 53, 61-62, 64, 81, 84-86, 89, 99, 217, 234, 267, 295, 345, 607
Bible, The 26, 34, 35, 100, 183, 188, 200, 204, 210, 229, 277, 317, 330

Catholics 32, 49, 54, 71, 104, 107, 135, 154, 161, 163, 170, 171, 179, 213, 238, 242, 252, 253, 256, 257, 288, 301, 305, 308, 309, 314, 333, 336, 339, 363-365, 389, 424, 438, 443, 447, 455, 458, 460, 475, 485, 497, 511, 518, 523, 532, 535, 541-544, 547, 552-555, 572-573, 575, 578, 584-586, 592, 594, 596, 597, 599, 600, 602, 604, 605, 610, 612, 613, 626-629, 640, 677-678, 682, 684, 686, 694, 696
Civil Religion 1, 5, 9, 23, 27, 60, 124-126, 164, 225, 279, 299, 300, 326, 338, 676

Democrats 88, 430, 431, 454, 466, 473, 475, 483, 494, 530, 534
Disciple of Christ 153, 157, 158

Episcopalians 189, 207, 212, 221, 244, 248, 622, 624, 636, 641, 643, 647, 667
Evangelicals 69, 76, 87, 421, 429, 445, 448, 464, 500-502, 525, 533

Fundamentalists 462, 469, 476, 514, 528-530

Graham, Billy 23, 131, 401, 410, 411, 416

Inaugural Address 16, 19, 27, 112, 142, 145

Jews 440, 441, 445, 456, 457, 461, 468, 471, 474, 479-481, 484, 515, 517, 531-532, 545, 577, 581-582, 609, 614, 644, 649, 670, 672, 673, 681

Methodists 321, 548, 619, 659

141

National Day of Prayer   7

Presbyterians   42-44, 175, 280, 307, 328, 620, 685, 692
Presidential Prayer Breakfast   14-15, 391
Protestants   108, 159, 250, 543, 585, 604, 612

Quakers   163, 165, 166, 168, 169, 172, 173, 390, 403, 621

Religious Liberty   110, 185, 194, 201, 202, 213, 223, 230, 236, 244, 246, 248, 249, 380, 383, 385, 616
Religious Right   448, 452, 470, 482, 505
Republicans   422, 432, 433, 435, 437, 444

Separation of Church and State   19, 219, 381

Unitarians   38, 195, 201, 203, 574, 576

Vatican, The   263, 438, 543, 544, 555, 572-573, 584, 585, 592, 594-597, 599-600, 602, 604-605, 612, 696